Mary Elle

YOU
HAVE WHAT
IT TAKES

Success Strategies for
Women at Work

You Have What It Takes

Published by Women Rising
Copyright © 2019 by Mary Ellen Connelly

ISBN: 978-1-7045160-2-8

maryellenconnelly.com
 AuthorMaryEllenConnelly
 @ME_Connelly

Editorial development and creative design support by Ascent:
www.spreadyourfire.net

The stories shared here are true.
Names and some identifying details have been
changed to protect the parties involved.

INTRODUCTION

I RACED IN FROM THE SCHOOL BUS to show Dad my report card. "Look, Dad, straight A's!" I looked eagerly up at him, only to see a carefully composed frown and then, "You do all right. . .for a girl."

Now it was my turn to frown and stomp my foot. "Da-aad!" Only then did he smile at me, as if I were in on the joke. I was not amused.

But maybe he knew what he was doing. Maybe he knew that being a smart girl would not be enough. That having that fighting spirit and a little righteous indignation would be needed to really find success in what was still "a man's world."

Maybe he was trying to see what was in me—besides head smarts—that would help me to succeed in life and the working world.

I loved math and science, so I decided on a career in engineering—before it was trendy for girls to be in STEM fields. Having grown up in a house full of boys, I had no issues with being the rare female in my engineering classes.

I knew I had it in me to succeed. **That belief would be challenged, as it is for many—maybe most—smart, capable women.**

I entered the workforce fully expecting to be treated equally, but I was not prepared for the obstacles that would come my way. I thought that surely doing my job well would get me the same recognition as anyone else. When I discovered that a male colleague with less experience, education, and responsibility was making more than I was, I immediately went to management. I was sure that once I pointed this out, they would fix it. I was wrong.

When my boss interrupted my technical briefing to comment on my earrings, I was thrown off balance—then left doubting myself because I had let this bother me. Whether boldly or subtly, there are so many things that can undermine us in the workplace.

When I was denied a promotion because I had children at home, I got angry. My strategy had to change, and I moved on. In fact, all along the way I had to create strategies to work around obstacles in my path—all the while holding onto the knowledge of my worth and helping others to recognize my value to the company.

Let me be clear about something at the outset. Though many of us women face challenges on the job *just because* we're women, this is not a book that focuses primarily on strategies to win over our male counterparts.

When the women in one office turned against me, I was shocked. But there it was: woman against woman competition.

This book is about helping you to survive and thrive at work despite obstacles, and to achieve whatever success at work may mean for you. Knowing how to do the job itself is often not enough: learning to strategize takes you the rest of the way.

Personal Challenges

I have had to endure the "million paper cuts" of being ignored, dismissed, and harassed—and not let any of it take me down.

In my 30+ years of experience in the male-dominated professions of engineering and high-tech sales, I've been through a lot—and succeeded anyway. I am proud of what I have accomplished. But more than that, I am passionate about helping other women find their own inner resources that lead to success. I wrote this book to help women learn not only from my experiences and insights gained but also from the women profiled here.

As I interviewed women for this book, I was amazed at the determination and savvy shown as we found our way to achieve our personal definition of success and accomplishment. Not everyone wants to be CEO, but we all want to feel valued and appreciated. We all want to be paid what we are worth and to have opportunities to move up. We want to have a voice and a place where our ideas are listened to and respected. We want our contributions to be recognized, and we want to look with pride at our accomplishments.

At the same time, I was saddened by what so many of us have had to endure. There is rarely a straight path to the top of our game, whatever that may be. The dozen women whose stories I share here learned to be strategists in a world still hostile to our positions in the workplace. We work in many different fields: law, engineering, marketing, information technology (IT), sales, human resources, and healthcare. Some started in supportive families and others in unsupportive ones. Some of us had children, and we worked while raising them. We've all faced and dealt with crises and blockages in the course of our careers.

Between us, we have been denied promotions because of having children or for refusing the sexual advances of our superiors. We have had projects and jobs taken from us and given to a man with no explanation, or we were sabotaged by other women who perceived us as a threat. We have been told to wear short skirts to meet with clients or were excluded from the boys' clubs at executive levels. We have suffered outrageous indignities, small slights, and blatant opposition. We have sometimes failed and always learned.

And yet we have adapted, changed, and developed into powerful, successful women on our own terms.

The thing is, you have what it takes to succeed and get the respect you deserve at work. What it takes is a deep desire to use the skills you possess naturally and those you have gained through training and experience. To these things, you can add or bolster other skills that are highlighted and explored in the pages that follow. You can learn to . . .

>> Recognize when you become a threat to others (male or female) and find ways to defuse the threat or deal with it.

>> Be aware of the tactics used against you and develop strategies to respond.

>> Leverage your strengths and improve your areas of weakness to achieve your goals.

>> Develop awareness of the world around you and others' motivations, finding the win-win approaches to dealing with them.

>> Learn to seek help and understand how to get others to do what you need.

>> Explore the laws and options for responding when discrimination or harassment occur.

>> Make your own rules, sometimes defying traditional female roles and bucking the status quo without guilt.

» Fight back when it's warranted or play the game, when that's the better choice.

» Change the game, when neither fighting nor playing along makes sense.

» Keep your cool under fire, recognizing self-defeating thoughts and behaviors, and replacing them with more empowering ones.

» Look for the positive in situations and avoid dwelling on the negative.

» Pick yourself up after every setback and move on.

Most important, when all is said and done: you will understand how to define personal success in your own terms and move toward your goals with eager determination.

And while this book is about finding your own level of success, it is also about helping you to believe in yourself. You do have what it takes to succeed—and now you can add to that the experiences and strategies shared here.

Because no one should have to settle for a serious message of "You do all right. . .for a girl."

CHAPTER 1

WOMEN AS A THREAT TO THE STATUS QUO

YOU KNOW A LOT, because you've experienced a lot. You have know-how, insight, great ideas, and maybe a good bit of life wisdom, too. All of this makes you a savvy woman.

It also makes you a threat.

How to be a threat to the status quo: Question unfair treatment

The first time I felt that being a smart woman was a threat—or at least the first time I recognized it as such—I was a young engineer working for a defense contractor in Northern Virginia. In the five years since graduating from college with an electrical engineering degree, I had established myself as a top-performing engineer in my company. Most recently, I had co-written a winning multi-million-dollar proposal for a hardware and software project, and was lead systems engineer and deputy program manager for this complex program—the largest in the Systems Engineering Group. I was also working toward my master's degree in electrical engineering, with only a few classes to go for completion. In a note celebrating my five-year anniversary with the company, Doug, the vice president who had hired me, told me, "I was high on your capabilities then and am even higher now." I loved my job and believed myself to be a valued asset for my company.

Then I got wind that Joey—a colleague of mine working on a smaller project—with less experience, responsibility, and education than me—was making a significantly higher salary than I: 20% more. It didn't make sense. My first instinct, knowing how important I was to the company, was that this was a mistake. *They must not realize that this discrepancy is there*, I naively thought.

Fighting back

I marched right in to see my boss. Bill was a kindly older gentle-man, retired military, who had been supportive of me since he was hired as my manager a few years prior when Doug was promoted. He had given me glowing performance reviews and increasing responsibility through the years. In one recent review, he praised my "flawless" writing skills and "extraordinary" technical abilities. Saying I had "exceeded all expectations" for professional growth, he recommended me for promotion and program management duties. Surely Bill would have my back. This was a very naive assumption.

The conversation started out awkwardly, as I tried to explain how I had found out Joey's salary while not compromising the person who had told me. Bill's face reddened a little as I spoke, though when he broke eye contact, I realized it was more from em-barrassment than anger.

"Mary Ellen, you know how important you are to me and to the company," he started slowly, looking straight at me. "I noticed the discrepancy in Joey's and your salaries when I was hired on, after I got to know your abilities, and I have been trying to fix it." He looked down at his hands, which were fidgeting with his pen on the desk. "But I only have so much leeway with salary to hand out. Since Joey is doing a good job, I can't not give him a raise, so it is taking some time to correct the disparity." He looked up at me, eyes beseeching me to accept this explanation.

I watched him, trying to separate in my mind the respect and affection I had for him from what he was saying. He was admitting the salary treatment was unfair but telling me he couldn't fix it. He didn't have the leeway to make the change. Twenty percent was a big difference. I needed to think.

"Thank you for acknowledging that the salary is inequitable," I told him, watching his eyes widen as he realized what he had said. "Please give this some thought, and we can talk more about it tomorrow." With that I walked away, fists clenched at my sides.

Struggling with the response

As I thought about it that evening, I couldn't sit still. I stomped around the house, thoughts raging in my head as I tried to understand what was happening. I had been so naive, assuming that my accomplishments, dedication, and hard work were appreciated and fairly rewarded. I had heard about women being paid less than men, of course, but I had assumed this was because of the types of jobs they were in. I didn't consider that in the same company, industry, and education level, a man would be paid more than a woman who had more experience, education, and responsibility. This feeling that they valued him more than me—after I had helped bring in the largest contract in the company and was lead systems engineer on that contract—was like a punch in the gut. I gave in to self-pity for a few moments, before the anger made me grit my teeth. This was a load of crap.

I took some time to make an objective assessment of the situation—always important. Responses made in the middle of an emotional flood tend to be and sound emotional; objectivity is critical.

Not only had Bill acknowledged that the salary difference was unfair but also that it had been that way for years, as he tried to slowly narrow the gap through slightly larger raises for me than Joey. I decided they owed me not only an adjustment to my current salary but also some reimbursement for being underpaid the past few years. However, as I thought about telling Bill that, I realized he wasn't the problem. He had been my supporter and mentor, recognizing my achievements and providing me with opportunities and increasing responsibility. The pay gap was there before he was hired. He was trying to fix it, but his hands were tied. I needed to take this up the chain if I wanted to get anywhere.

Escalating

The next day, I asked Bill to join me, and we walked in to the director's office and sat down across from Dick. I got right to the point.

"I have discovered that I am being paid inequitably, and I would like to discuss how we can fix that." Dick looked confused, and I realized Bill had not told him about our previous discussion. Bill squirmed in his seat, offering nothing.

"I found out that Joey is making a significantly higher salary than me. As you know, he has less experience, less education, and less responsibility than I." Dick interrupted, "How did you find that out?" aiming his narrowed eyes first at me, then at Bill.

Knowledge is power.
Power can be a threat.

When a woman has knowledge and insights into what is happening at a company, she gains power—and becomes a threat to those who want to maintain the status quo.

Everything was going swimmingly—according to my company—when I was doing more work for less pay and didn't know about it. My finding out made me a major threat to the status quo. Dick was very unhappy about this.

Salaries are generally kept secret at companies for a lot of very good reasons and a few not-so-good ones. Knowing what your colleagues are making can be very disruptive for morale. If there is a major pay gap between management and workers—even when it is industry standard practice and based on responsibility and education and experience—those making less can take it hard. But this secrecy can also be a breeding ground for unfair salary treatment as in my case.

My gaining knowledge about the discrepancy and confronting it directly put me in a pitted battle with a company that didn't want to be called on its unfair practices.

It would not be the last time in my career.

The struggle is real—it's not a joke

What lies ahead for you as an accomplished woman is still, sad to say, struggle—maybe even a war. Yes, women are making strides, but there is still resistance. In historically male-dominated professions, women are challenging the status quo and need to fight to move ahead. Even in more typically female professions, women face obstacles when they try to move up in their careers. Savvy women are being promoted above men and other women, both of which groups may resent the change and feel their egos threatened. Mothers are working to stay on track with their careers—upsetting the status quo both at work and in their families and communities. Men comfortable with their male colleagues are unhappy finding their behavior is not acceptable in a mixed workplace—and perhaps the new woman is to blame. As women gain knowledge and power, they can become a threat to the egos of those around them—and suddenly find themselves targets, battling tactics aimed to bring them back down.

There are ways to win the struggle and move toward where you need to go. That's what this book is about.

First, we need to be shrewd about how entrenched the forces of the status quo can be.

It gets worse

"It wasn't Bill that told me, and I'd prefer not to say how I found out. What's important here is that I know, and Bill tells me he has been trying to make adjustments to the salary gap but is limited by management on what can be done."

At this point, Dick's steely eyes aimed back at Bill, who continued to squirm but kept quiet, waiting to see how this would play out. The strength in my voice masked the butterflies in my stomach as I continued. "I would like to get an out-of-cycle pay increase to close the gap. Frankly, I feel like you owe me more than that, since this has been going on for a while, but I will settle for making our salaries equal." I sat back in my chair and waited, watching Dick's knitted brow and red face.

He studied me for a moment and then looked away. "Now, Mary Ellen, you need to just calm down." The syrupy sweetness in his voice made me want to slap him, as he looked back at me with a manufactured look of concern.

"Of course we value your contributions, but you don't realize how much value Joey brings to the table? His customer has a lot of respect for him over at the lab. It's not just about experience and education, you know. I'm sure Bill would agree." He looked over at Bill with daggers in his eyes. Bill nodded slowly. He was in enough trouble already. But his reddening face and inability to look at me told me he didn't really believe what Dick was saying.

As Dick continued to talk about how great Joey was, my stomach sank, and I stopped listening. I realized they had no intention of correcting my pay. Dick felt he was right in paying Joey a higher salary and was going to find plenty of reasons to justify it. Never mind that I had "exceeded all expectations." As long as salaries were kept quiet, they could pay me less and get more. I was a bargain.

By confronting them with the issue, however, I was now a threat.

Now what?

Could I have done something different with my knowledge of the pay discrimination? Were there strategies I could have used to support my case or others I should have consulted? Probably, but I was still young and figuring things out. I'm sure putting Bill in the middle and catching him off guard in front of his manager, Dick, was not the smartest move. At that point, I lost him as an ally. I was strong but not willing to fight what was looking like a losing battle. I had not yet developed the savvy I would need to negotiate this terrain, but it was a learning experience.

In the end, no adjustments were made to my pay. I now knew how they felt about my contributions, and my loyalty to the company dropped as well. Within a few months, I sought and accepted a job elsewhere, hoping that my skills would be more valued by another company.

Accept that you're going to be a threat to someone

Studies and statistics document well that women continue to make less money than men and face many biases in the workplace. This occurs at all levels of society and in nearly all industries, though it may be greater in typically male-dominated careers such as engineering, computer science/IT, military, law enforcement, and law.

Here's the thing: when intelligent, ambitious women strive to change the status quo, challenge male-dominated companies, compete on a level playing field, and achieve what is rightfully ours, we are very likely to become a threat.

Look at the situation I was in more closely, and you'll see the anatomy of what occurs when you pair your knowledge with something else you possess—personal power. As women, we need our power as well as our knowledge, because we can find ourselves on a playing field—or even a field of battle—where strength is needed. Whether we intend it or not, others can see us not just as adults using our insight and knowledge but as adversaries.

It may seem that when I questioned my salary's being lower than Joey's, I became a threat to management, because there were laws about equal pay, and they were afraid they were "caught." Certainly there is some truth to that. Even back then, in the mid-1980s, laws were on the books to protect against such discrimination.

But stepping back, there were larger forces at play. Why was the salary difference there in the first place, and why did they feel the need to defend it rather than fix it? More than 20 years after the passage of the Equal Pay Act (more on this in Chapter Six), these men felt justified in paying a woman a lower salary than a man, even though she did *more* than he. This was the way it was; they were comfortable with it and wanted to keep it that way. In questioning management's decisions and exposing the discrepancy, I became a threat to the status quo that women could be paid less than men.

Knowing you are a threat is one thing; learning to accept it is another. It takes experience—and confidence in yourself—to own your power. I didn't like knowing that I was paid less for doing more and that my value was somehow less than Joey's because I was a woman, or for whatever other reason they could come up with. I knew my own worth, and I parlayed it into a higher salary at a new company.

Becoming a threat: Be the first female in a typically male role

Though it may seem that glass ceilings have been broken, they still exist. We still see women breaking through to become the first in a typically male role. This does not sit well with everyone.

The salary issue was not the only time I would find myself threatening the status quo based solely on the fact that I was a strong woman. As I progressed in my career, I noticed there were no women in positions above me. As I strove to move up, I found myself again threatening the status quo of only men in management roles. The tactics used to keep me and other women from moving up and ahead were astounding.

Valerie, a young woman in a man's world

Valerie broke ground throughout her career as she rose up through the ranks from computer operator to chief information officer (CIO)—she was often the first female in her roles. She encountered great opposition as she challenged the status quo of this male-dominated industry. According to Valerie:

My whole career has been in this man's world of IT. In 1975 when we were in class, 90% of the students in my college programming classes were men. When I was in computer operations, I was the first female computer operator they ever hired, because they didn't think a woman could do the job. I was 19 at the time. I was a real threat, because they realized *Oh, a woman can do the job. Now we have to hire other women?* They didn't like that. They wanted me to come in to fail so they could prove women couldn't do that. It didn't work.

Recognize it's not just men who resent our upward mobility

Frequently women find themselves a threat to other women as much as they are to men. Often women are more comfortable working for men, and they resent it when a woman is promoted or hired above them.

When I moved to sales and marketing manager in a small company some years later, I was the first woman in a management role. There were female engineers at the company working on projects in different departments, and the other women were in support roles. I was surprised to find these women resented me and didn't like "taking orders" or doing tasks given them by another woman. I was again a threat to the status quo.

All the women I interviewed experienced almost as much resistance from women in the workplace as they did from men. Whether this is caused by jealousy or just plain discomfort with change, it affects us all.

Try to change long-held behaviors and culture

Many women find their role to be a direct threat to the status quo, because their job includes ensuring the company follows the law and keeps the work environment free from harassment and discrimination. These smart women in Human Resources and other departments often find themselves in the line of fire when they try to implement change or enforce rules within the company even though that is what they were hired to do.

When Karen moved from working in government consulting startups to working in Human Resources with a large automotive group with multiple dealerships, she faced a dramatic culture shift— and realized her services were greatly needed. She encountered many examples of sexual harassment and other unethical/illegal behaviors in the dealerships. Her role was to protect the company and its employees, and as a result, she advised the CEO to fire even top-performing, longstanding employees who were violating rules that put the company at risk. The very nature of her job was a threat to the status quo.

Pressing for change unsettles the status quo

Even if your role is not in Human Resources, you may find the workplace culture to be hostile to or uncomfortable for women. By insisting on being treated with respect and having your contributions valued, you rock the boat. If you further want to avoid hearing profanity or screaming or viewing inappropriate pictures on the wall or on someone's computer, you are threatening the status quo.

When Lynn, a smart and outspoken engineer, moved from the Navy to another government organization, she challenged the way things were. She found the new environment full of "yes men" and women—which can be typical of organizations led by former military officers who are not used to being questioned. When she spoke up during meetings or questioned decisions being made, she was branded a troublemaker. "There's a big "group think" thing going. If you don't act or think like them, you are an island." Lynn was more inclined to ask questions, discuss options, and generally help problem-solve on usual engineering practices. This did not go over well. When she was asked to work on a new project, she was told not to express her opinion. She had become a threat to the culture of the organization.

A successful woman must be a *strong* woman if she wants to keep moving forward.

How?

You begin by learning what to do and what not to do. In this book, you will hear our stories and how we have reached our own success in spite of the crap we have encountered in our careers. You can learn from our successes and our mistakes. You will learn what laws are there to protect you and how to claim your own personal power. You will see how we recover from defeat, negotiate around obstacles, and define our own paths forward.

And then you get to apply it to your own life. You look around and figure out if and where you have become a threat and how you can deal with that. You examine your own career successes and failures, and your strengths and weaknesses, and make adjustments as needed based on what you have learned. You start from where you are now, and you find a way to move your career in the direction you want. You are in control of how you deal with obstacles. You are in control of your own career. You have what it takes. Own it.

CHAPTER 2

TACTICS USED AGAINST YOU: THE SIX "D's"

AT SOME LEVEL, IT HARDLY MATTERS why a woman has become a threat, though it certainly helps to understand the reasons. The real issue comes when the "threatened" parties take action—using tactics against a woman to bring her down or keep her from moving up.

These tactics can range from very subtle to outrageous and all levels in between. As I said before, anyone can be perceived threat to anyone else—man or woman—but the tactics used against women are often specifically targeted at her gender. I call them the six D's: dismiss, disparage, disconcert, dissemble, discriminate, and dishearten. Individually, they may seem harmless, but when taken as a whole, they can wreak enormous damage on a woman's psyche and career.

Dismiss

Frequently women will find themselves or their ideas simply dismissed, brushed away like so much lint on someone's shoulder. As if you were not important enough to even be listened to. Whether this is part of the corporate culture or the tactic of one or more colleagues or managers, an experienced woman recognizes the behavior and finds ways to be taken seriously.

Ignoring your input/making you invisible

The problem is pervasive even in today's society. Women are made to feel unimportant even in making purchasing decisions with their own money.

Several years ago, I brought a male friend on a vacation to a place where I owned a timeshare—purchased on my own years before. We attended the "owner update" together, where they purportedly tell you how best to use your membership, but in reality, they try to sell you more points. The ownership is in my name, and we explained that from the outset. My friend was simply along for the company. That didn't stop the salesman from addressing his entire sales pitch and all questions directly to my friend. It was as if I didn't exist. I didn't buy anything he was selling.

This has happened to me and no doubt to countless women when buying cars, houses, computers, financial services, televisions, and many other items or services. Getting a salesperson to look me in the eye and take me seriously is nearly impossible if I have a man with me. Even if I go alone, I've been asked "Does your husband approve?" or generally been dismissed as someone not likely to make a decision that day.

These experiences are less likely to be tactics in keeping women from being a threat—more likely they are just bad sales tactics. Yet they are still pervasive in society and make it easy for men to use the same tactics with women they work with. As frustrating as it is to be dismissed in the marketplace, it can be even more so—and detrimental to a woman's career—to be similarly disregarded in the workplace.

The easiest way to take away a woman's power is to assume she doesn't have any to begin with.

All the women I interviewed have felt themselves, or their ideas, dismissed in the workplace at one time or another. For Shirley and Karen, in Human Resources roles in very different industries, it was a way of life. Even as Shirley rose through the ranks to HR director (in the top 1% of a 100,000-person company), HR was considered a support role. She was expected to go along with whatever the managers, directors, and vice president (VPs) (all generally men) wanted her to do. If she proposed an idea in a meeting, she would receive a blank stare, a silent pause, and then someone else would quickly change the subject. Later, if a man repeated her idea, possibly slightly rephrased, people would jump on it and tell him what a great idea he had.

Karen has had similar issues with feeling dismissed, both early in her career working for small government contractors, and now in her role working in HR for an automotive group. According to Karen, when she would suggest an idea, "What if we do this and move this over here?" the response would be, "Okay, thanks for sharing;" then they would look away.

Dismissed again. Why bother trying?

When you are dismissed, you feel like you've been kicked in the gut. After you're kicked in the gut enough times, you tend not to keep trying.

Eventually, Shirley stopped putting forth her ideas or found other ways to get them implemented while still receiving no credit. Karen also learned to play the game, feeding ideas to men and then pouncing on them with "Great idea!" when they brought them up in meetings. Neither option made the women feel valued, even if they were ultimately able to get ideas implemented. And motivation takes a big hit. What is the cost to organizations when this happens?

Or you can push back

You can make a lot of noise when you feel you are being dismissed and not let them take you down easily. Remind them that you do have personal power, and they can't just ignore you.

Rosa, a successful attorney and recognized expert in her specific field of law, is less likely to sit back quietly when she feels dismissed. When her current law firm launched a new web site, adding the capabilities for her area of expertise, they failed to list her name as one of the attorneys in that practice. "I've written books every year on that area of the law, all my business is there, and yet my clients can't find me on the web site? I call 'bullshit'!" She fought to get her name listed.

Not taking you seriously/ talking only to the men in the room

Often the expectation is that women won't be contributing much, and people who don't know better will talk only to the men in the room or ask them for confirmation of what you are saying.

When I first started noticing men in meetings acknowledging or supporting only the other men, I didn't think anything of it. Generally, I was the only woman or one of a few, and as a junior engineer, I understood that my ideas were less valued. That didn't stop me from speaking up, however. As I gained more technical knowledge and program management responsibility, and a master's degree in my field, I expected the same level of respect as my male colleagues. I was surprised to find myself still ignored. Not that I wasn't noticed—the only female in a room full of men tends to stand out—but when I expressed an opinion or technical nuance, they would nod and smile and then look to one of the male engineers on my team for confirmation.

Short of waving your arms around so they know you are there, keep your head in the game. Keep putting out your ideas, interrupt the men if need be, and get yourself noticed. It's not always easy to do, but it will pay off if you persist.

Instead of becoming frustrated with this, Becky and one of her colleagues made it a kind of game. Young, attractive, and highly qualified IT professionals, they found they could get meetings with clients easily—possibly not based on their qualifications. "When we walked in, people would look up and say, 'Are you kidding me?' but then we would open our mouths. Jennifer would take engineers to the mat: she had a master's degree in electrical engineering, and she had ridiculous certifications. She was trained on all the switches, routers, etc. When you got into bits and bytes and what integrated with what, she was on it. And it was a riot; it got so bad you would dress for it. 'Fine. You want to play?' We would be in the parking lot, putting on skirts and heels. 'Ready?' Walk in there with fresh gloss, powdered nose. Not flirty but dressed in our best suits and heels. 'We are here to talk to you about this.' We could tell we had gotten in, because it would be fun for them. By the end, they would buy from us, because we had passed the test."

At some point, if you don't let them get to you, they may learn you have something to say.

"Boys' club"/exclusion

I know, it's a cliché. Really, does the "boys' club" still exist? Hell, yes, it does. And it's an effective tactic to keep a woman from gaining too much power.

Judy, an IT professional at a telecommunications company, continued to work hard and progress through the ranks, and she was promoted to a high-level role: technical director reporting directly to the chief technology officer (CTO). Judy was a key part of the technical team, helping to influence the direction of decisions made by the CTO.

Judy was the only female among the CTO's staff, and she started to get the sense they didn't know what to do with a woman at her level. When her colleagues and boss got together after work for beers, she was not invited, as the casual get-togethers were billed as "guys only." But they were talking about business when they were out, making decisions, and building relationships. Judy, with a family waiting for her at home, didn't particularly want to go to these, but she felt like being excluded from these networking opportunities was holding her career back.

She also discovered she was being excluded from important communications among her team, leaving her less informed and unable to respond quickly to urgent matters.

Had Judy's presence in higher levels in the company made it awkward for some "boys' club" to continue? When she walked into a room, and the conversation stopped, was it simply because they were telling an inappropriate joke, or was more important information being passed that she was not privy to? Whether the others on the team considered Judy a threat to their own promotion possibilities, a threat to their comfort level in working with an all-male team, or just a threat to the status quo, they were finding ways to exclude her and make it more challenging for her to move ahead.

All these dismissal tactics are used against women generally to keep us in our places. We have become a threat to the status quo or to someone's ego, and by dismissing us, they can take away our power. We have been ignored, overlooked, and outright excluded from important business meetings.

Clever women find ways to be seen and heard.

Disparage: A destructive D

To disparage someone is to regard or represent her as being of little worth. If a woman has become a threat, a very effective tactic can be to discredit her, undervalue her contributions, or question her competence.

Several of the women I interviewed and I have suffered some form of disparagement—from having our reputations trashed behind our backs or our competence questioned outright. This can present challenges, especially if you don't know what is being said and by whom.

Trashing your reputation behind your back

Even if you find out someone is talking badly about you without your knowledge, you can have a lot of difficulty pinpointing the problem and solving it.

One of Lynn's top managers called her into his office to discuss a problem.

"Lynn, I heard a couple things about you and want to talk with you about it. People have come to me and said you're mean."

"I'm mean? Who said that?"

"I can't tell you."

"Okay, give me examples."

"Sure. When you're sitting in engineering review boards, you never smile. I'm a guy; if I don't smile they just think I'm a hard ass. You? They think you're a bitch. I know it's a double standard, but can you just start smiling more at meetings?"

Lynn looked at him. "When I'm in a meeting, I'm thinking. I'm not going to interrupt my thinking to put a dumb smile on my face to make some insecure person feel better."

She recognized that he was telling her this to try to help her, even knowing it's a double standard. But he was very serious. At the next couple of meetings, she watched and noticed some of the women smiling the whole time—though not contributing to the conversation. Lynn told me, "It would really distract me to try to do that."

Even if the accusation leveled against you is ridiculous, it can damage your reputation.

Rosa has also had issues with others talking poorly of her behind her back—especially those whom she had proven wrong or argued with about a legal issue. Egos threatened, they fought back by telling others she was inconsistent. "You never know what Rosa you're gonna get—the Rosa that's technically strong or the Rosa that shoots from the hip." According to Rosa:

> The difference between being a tax lawyer and being a litigator is that when you are on the tax side, the government gives you very specific instructions. My area of the law develops in the courts. So no, I wasn't shooting from the hip. I was saying, "Well, that's a question that is very difficult to answer

because the courts are split. Depending on the juris-
diction you are in, it could go this way, that way, or
somewhere in the middle. If my recollection serves
me correctly, I think it's this, but I'm not sure,
because right now I'm not on your client's clock,
because you didn't say 'Bill it.' You're just walking
into my office wanting my gut reaction. So when
that asshole goes around saying 'You never know
which Rosa you're gonna get,' oh, no. I'm pretty sure
that when you walked into my office and I wasn't
asked to bill it, you just wanted my opinion. You are
going to get the shoot-from-the-hip Rosa. I figured
you wanted to be educated, because I have written
and updated a book on the topic since 1996. Let me
explain something to you, stupid asshole, I can run
rings around you on these issues. Now, 'shoot from
the hip'? Fuck yourself."

Questioning your competence

Sometimes the attacks are even more direct. In Chapter 11, you will
read about Connie's dentist employer rebuking her in front of a patient, snatching away the instrument and saying "I'll be the judge
of that"—or later, Connie's colleague screaming at her, "What the
hell do you know? You're just a woman." When Sheila's manager
(Chapter 15) took away the project she built from scratch, he sent
the message that he didn't believe she was capable of running the
program.

Any time someone questions your competence, it hurts. Even if
you know you are more than capable, it can instill doubt in yourself

and in others. The best recourse is to quickly assess whether the accusation is valid and push back if it's not.

Disconcert—causing you discomfort

Many of us have encountered disconcerting attacks when we find ourselves in a situation where we are a threat to others. This generally comes in the form of their finding our vulnerabilities and pushing on them.

When I was up for a promotion years ago, and my manager wanted to give it to my male colleague, he pushed back on me by focusing on my "working mother guilt." He thought that if he pushed hard enough, explaining that the job would require long hours and travel and an inability to accommodate my children's schedule, I would drop my application rather than choose between work and family.

When Shirley's company reorganized and brought another woman in as her manager, the new woman was threatened by Shirley's strong connections and experience within the division. She launched multiple tactics against Shirley, including withholding information and keeping her off key teams. Then she would pull Shirley aside and tell her, "Your colleagues are worried about you,"— refusing to provide further details on who had said what. According to Shirley, "It was crazy-making. I had never in my career gotten that kind of negative feedback, and there was not enough detail for me to refute the claims."

Dissemble—the tricky one

To dissemble is to give a false or misleading appearance, to conceal one's true motives, or to speak or act hypocritically. Many of the women I interviewed have encountered this type of behavior in the workplace, either directly or indirectly.

Promotion without power

One example of this is promotion without power. Rosa and Diana saw it frequently within their law firms, when less-qualified attorneys would be promoted to partner because they could be controlled by the other partners.

In my case, after proving myself as program manager on a multi-million-dollar program, I was promoted to Engineering Department manager. Putting a female in this type of role was a first for my company—and not entirely a comfortable decision all around. When the new organization chart came out, I was indeed Engineering Department manager with 20 engineers reporting to me, most of them men, several of them older than I. I had just turned 30.

But I noticed something odd on the org chart. A new box, just under the director and off to the side, called "Technical Staff." Two names were listed: Tom, a senior engineer who had been my technical mentor and coworker on my program for many years, and Joey, who was one year younger than I, and who (I had previously discovered) was making more money than I was.

Why were these two engineers pulled out of the department just as I took on the role of manager? Was I somehow less qualified to manage them than the rest of the team? Or was there something else at work here? Of course, it's quite likely that they didn't want me to see the higher pay of these two engineers. Tom's higher pay was completely valid, as he had many years more experience than I. He also would have had no issue working for me, as he had no desire to be in management and had a lot of respect for me. Joey was likely still paid more than I for doing less, and they wouldn't want me in charge of his raises. They couldn't have an org chart box with just his name, so Tom got to join him in the Technical Staff.

Passive-aggressive support

When I was sales and marketing manager at a small engineering company, I was surprised to encounter opposition from the women supporting me. I suspect they didn't like taking direction from another woman . . . and I say I "suspect" this, because they never outright refused to do something for me. They would smile sweetly and say "Of course," then quietly forget to do it or do it poorly, making me look bad.

When Anne was a paralegal, she had a secretary who was a little older than she, who did not like doing work for her. The secretary would either refuse to do the work outright or say she would do it and then drop it. When Anne's supervisor confronted the secretary and told her she would have to do work for Anne, she quit.

Discriminate—it's still happening

Discrimination still exists in many forms, both blatant and subtle. It is frequently used in response to a woman who has become a threat to the status quo or to the ego of someone in the workplace.

Because you are a woman

Working mothers often find the most blatant discrimination disguised in the form of caring about how you balance your work and family life. When Judy was pregnant with her second child, her manager told her she wouldn't be recommending her for a new team leader position in her company. According to her manager, "You would have gotten the role, but with your going on maternity leave soon, we didn't think the timing was right for you."

Valerie had similar issues when she was raising her youngest son. She discovered she was not being recommended for projects because she had a baby at home—even though she was willing and able to do the work. According to Valerie, "I find people will make decisions about somebody—whether they are ready for a job, a promotion, whatever. If they know something is going on in their personal life, they'll say, 'Oh, they shouldn't take that on. That's just more stress; they don't need that.'"

Sometimes the simple fact of being female can limit you, for reasons you might not even know about. Karen and Rosa both witnessed discussions and decisions being made about women up for hiring or promotion where the following statements were made:

"You can't hire her, because she is beautiful and will distract the men."

"You can't promote her, because they won't want to work for a woman."

"I can't hire her—my wife would be pissed! Find me someone ugly."

Because you will pick up their slack

Often women get stuck in a position because they are willing to take care of the dirty work and take up the slack of others who have let things slide. Sheila built a hugely successful program at one of her earlier jobs, putting in long hours and doing most of the work herself. When it came time for appointing a director of the program she had built, they hired a man from the outside and moved her onto another project.

At another job later in her career, Sheila had implemented a manual billing process and was doing all the billing herself. This continued long past when it made sense to do manual billing, but they had no incentive to fix it, because she was doing the work.

Because we are trained from a young age to allow it

This tendency seems to start early. I recently spoke to a young woman doing an internship at a local technology firm. On her small project team, the others often do a sloppy job or leave things undone, knowing she will come in and clean it up to make the team look good—putting in long hours to make it happen. This is something of a Catch-22, because if you don't pick up the slack, the whole team looks bad, but it sets a precedent for being in that type of role for the long term.

Because you want to move up

Upward mobility for women is still much slower than for men; that's no secret. Even in industries where women are a majority of the workforce, men often dominate the management team.

Women in the Workplace 2016, a study conducted by LeanIn.org and McKinsey, reports, "Women remain underrepresented at every level in the corporate pipeline. Corporate America promotes men at 30 percent higher rates than women during their early career stages, and entry-level women are significantly more likely than men to have spent five or more years in the same role." As part of the study, 132 companies employing more than 4.6 million people shared their pipeline data and completed a survey of HR practices. In addition, 34,000 employees completed a survey designed to uncover their attitudes on gender, job satisfaction, ambition, and work-life issues.

Shirley found that women in her large defense contractor were becoming stuck at the project manager level and had trouble moving even to the director level. I bounced up against the glass ceiling at my first company, and I was barely standing up. All of us have seen it. Notice how many teachers are women and how many school administrators are men. Why is that?

Because you want to make as much money as your peers

Another widely known issue for women is the pay gap. In a report put out by the American Association of University Women (AAUW) titled *The Simple Truth About the Gender Pay Gap, Fall 2016 edition,* data from The Bureau of Labor Statistics and the Census Bureau show that women are paid, on average, 80% of what men are paid, a gap of 20%. Some of the difference is explained by occupational choices—where typically male-dominated jobs in construction, transportation, and engineering pay more than typically female occupations in health care, education, and administrative support. According to the study, "Even women in male-dominated jobs such as computer programming still face a pay gap compared with their male counterparts (19%), even though women in such jobs may be paid higher salaries than women in traditionally female fields are paid. . . .. Not all of the gender pay gap can be "explained away" by choices such as college major, occupation, work hours, and time out of the workforce. Discrimination and bias against women in the workplace are also culprits in the pay gap."

When I questioned why my salary was lower than that of a colleague with less education, experience, and responsibility than

I had, I was given a bullshit answer and no raise. Mostly, though, salaries are hidden from employees to avoid questioning. In the most progressive companies, systems are in place to try to prevent a huge wage disparity. But because so much of your value to a company is subjective, managers can skew reviews or give choice assignments to men to make them more upwardly mobile. Salary discrimination is alive and well.

Dishearten—taking away your will to fight

In our quest to work hard, contribute to our company and career, move up, and find satisfaction in our work, even the smallest things can sometimes be discouraging. Whether they are deliberate tactics against women or just a continuation of long-held practices, the combination of factors that dishearten women can destroy our drive and ability to move up.

Assigning you "female" roles

Nearly all of us have at one time or another been assigned a typically "female" role. How many times were we asked, as the only female in the room, to take notes in a meeting? The savviest of us find ways to get out of it.

Lynn had a guy come into a meeting that didn't know her. "He asked me where the sugar is and stuff. I said, 'Oh, it's right there. Do you need a cup?' The other guys were laughing. Then I ended up running the meeting, and he turned all shades of red."

Becky was appalled when a former manager insisted that one of her colleagues "put on a skirt to go to that meeting." Later that manager insisted Becky go work the booth at a trade show, because she was pretty and would attract men to the booth.

Even today, I see booths at technical trade shows deliberately manned by "booth babes," women hired to dress scantily and lure men to the booth. There is nothing wrong with taking notes, helping someone with coffee, or working at a booth in a trade show. But when you are trying to distinguish yourself on your technical skills or knowledge or hard work, standing out only because you are a woman is disheartening.

A million paper cuts—small things that set the tone

Along with the big things that hold women back, sometimes the small things set the tone and remind you that you are not in charge.

When Connie was a dental hygienist, she worked for Dr. Maxwell, an older man with a string of ex-wives and a temperament to explain it. When a male technician came in to inspect the X-ray machine, the receptionist asked him to wait until the current patient was finished. Dr. Maxwell overheard it and scolded her, "You do not keep Mr. Johnson waiting." As he ushered the confused technician back to the exam room, Connie heard Dr. M. say, "I've got to keep these girls in line." Though she should have been used to it by then, she still cringed when she heard him talk about his "girls."

Often the issue is not dramatic enough to be worth complaining about. Sometimes it just makes you crazy.

When I was manager of the Engineering Department, I stopped my director in the hall for a discussion of a technical issue on a large program I was running. Deep into the discussion, he interrupted my sentence to say, "Nice earrings." It completely derailed my train of thought and made me wonder if he was paying any attention to my technical discussion—or just checking me out.

Diana has encountered similar comments. In the midst of an intense conversation about the nuances of the law and the client, she was interrupted by her managing partner, who asked, "Did you change your hair?"

Mad Men is not just historical fiction

Blatant sexual harassment and innuendo still exist in some workplaces. When Karen first started at the automotive group, she was amazed at the amount of sexual harassment that was tolerated—and sometimes encouraged. Salesmen surfing pornography on the showroom floor, men making sexual and suggestive comments to female coworkers, excessive profanity, etc. In this type of environment, a woman would find it nearly impossible to be comfortable or to advance her career.

Seriously?

Several of us have been told to "calm down" when we are particularly passionate about an issue or problem. We have never heard anyone tell a male colleague to calm down, even when he was screaming at someone.

Surprisingly (or not), Valerie, Becky, Karen, and I have all heard on multiple occasions a version of "You sound like my wife!" or "You sound like my mother!" Valerie, a seasoned and highly competent professional, took it in stride. "Okay, if you want it like that. Sit down and listen to me."

These comments may seem innocuous, and in an even playing field, perhaps they would be. But this is not an even playing field. We may be women, but by putting us in a bucket with their wife or mother, men keep us from competing fairly with men. Who knows what sort of baggage they bring to the conversation when they think of us as like their wife? We've never heard Joe down the hall being compared to their father.

Don't let it get you down

An accomplished woman will become a threat to others, who will often react with conscious or unconscious actions against her. We have all faced various tactics used against us during our career progression. Some were more effective than others in slowing us down. Over time, however, we have developed strategies to fight back and prevail in spite of them.

The first step is recognizing what is happening. The most successful women . . .

» Recognize when we are being dismissed and insist on being heard. We own our own power.

» Don't let disparaging comments get us down. Savvy women challenge those who are trying to disparage us or—through continuous competence—simply prove them wrong.

» Are strong in the face of disconcerting attacks where others push on our vulnerabilities to try to break us. The more we recognize what is happening, the less power others have over us.

» Learn to recognize when dissembling is used to provide false appearances, such as promotion without power or passive-aggressive support. The more we know the true motives of others, the better strategies we can put in place to challenge these behaviors.

» Know that discrimination still exists. We recognize when we have become a threat to the status quo or to someone's ego, and we find ways to excel in spite of this. We continue to question the pay gap, and we insist on equal opportunities in promotions and training and growth paths.

» Are not disheartened by the large and small injustices we see in the workplace. We speak up when we see blatant sexual harassment and discrimination, and we learn to brush aside the minor comments that remind us that we are women in a (formerly) man's job. Or we stand up and say, "Pay attention. I'm speaking, and I have something important to say."

In the following chapters, we will explore different approaches you can use in responding to the challenges you will face. You will learn from our successes and our mistakes, finding your own way forward.

CHAPTER 3

KNOW YOUR STRENGTHS AND WEAKNESSES

YOU MAY BELIEVE that others are dismissing, criticizing, or overlooking you—just because you're a woman. Before you *decide* you're being treated unfairly, however, make *sure* that this is the case. A discerning woman takes time for a good self-assessment, knows her strengths and weaknesses, and sets her own goals for improvement.

Don't ignore your areas for improvement

I was always pretty good at knowing my strengths and leveraging them. I was smart, a good writer, and a leader. As a systems engineer and program manager, I had the ability to see the big picture (system design), how the details fit into it, and what needed to be done to make it all work. Writing came easily to me, so I was also good at quickly developing proposals or system documentation.

But I had a harder time recognizing my weaknesses. If anyone were to ask me about areas I could improve in—in an interview, for example—it felt like a trick question. Like I should say, "I work too hard," or "I care too much about the customer." I didn't really want to consider weaknesses in myself, and I surely didn't want to talk about them.

For years, the companies I worked for gave me glowing performance evaluations—recounting how awesome I was in every way. Evaluation time for me was a big stroke to my ego, and I felt like I could do anything.

It was only when I questioned my unfair salary treatment or put in for a promotion that my company suddenly came up with a list of areas in which I needed to improve. "Joey has great relationships with the customer"—and apparently that was an area I needed work on? "David has more experience with leading proposal teams and therefore will be more valuable in the new deputy director role."

If I had been savvier then, I would have been more aware of how others around me were doing and what the company valued in its employees. At a minimum, I should have looked closely at myself to see where I needed to improve in relation to my job and the company's expectations, and sought training or opportunities to shore those areas up. That way, even if my managers wanted to continue to discriminate, they would have a harder time justifying themselves.

Leverage your strengths

The first—and easiest—thing to figure out about yourself is where your strengths lie. Once you understand what your best skills are, you can seek opportunities that most need and value these skills. This is one of the surest ways to advance your career.

Take time to really examine and ask yourself these questions, or others relevant to your career path:

1. Do you work best as an individual contributor, as part of a team, or as a leader? Not everyone is cut out for every role, so the more you understand where you shine, the more you can seek these types of roles. Of course, becoming a CEO can take decades, so if you are a leader, find ways to lead within the scope of your responsibilities.

2. Are you a good writer? Don't underestimate the power of a well-formed sentence, regardless of your choice of careers. Even in engineering, I found that being able to write proposals or requirements documents was a hugely valuable asset. And if you are not a good writer, take some courses. Bad spelling and grammar will make you look much dumber than you really are and will hold you back.

3. Are you a big-picture person or detail oriented? Some people excel at detailed work, and others are better at understanding the big picture and how everything fits together within it. Thank goodness for all of them. Know which you are and seek opportunities where you best fit.

4. What specific skills in your industry are your strengths? This may be a bit of a no-brainer, because if I were an excellent C programmer, I probably

wouldn't seek work in embedded hardware design. But it's always a good exercise to list your best skills periodically, because they will change as your career evolves. One way to do this is to continue to update your resume, even if you are not seeking a new job. In addition to helping you focus your career growth, listing your accomplishments can be a big ego boost.

Once you have identified your strengths with these and other questions, you can be alert to opportunities to leverage them.

What about your passions?

Being good at something is well and good, but what if you hate doing it? What if you find that you are great at the fine details of keeping a spreadsheet up to date, but you would much rather be designing new ways to capture information and present it? Knowing your passions is as important as knowing your strengths and weaknesses.

Obviously, aligning your strengths with your passion is ideal, but that doesn't always work. We are all best at the things we love and more driven to improve in areas we need to if that will get us closer to realizing our goals.

Don't wait for others to tell you where you need to improve

If, in your company culture, people only tell you what you are doing right, make sure you are looking carefully at yourself to know how you can improve. Even if you receive regular feedback on your areas of improvement, be sure to look beyond that to truly understand your own weaknesses. It is ultimately your responsibility to get the skills and experience you need to move forward.

Anne: Argue from a position of power

A smart, strong, and opinionated attorney working for the federal government, Anne was never afraid to speak up when she saw something was wrong. First, she made sure her facts were straight and her case was solid.

> I didn't get promotions, because people who did get promotions were white males with children. I internalized that I wasn't smart enough, rather than any kind of discrimination. That's got to be what it is. I took affirmative actions—if I wasn't a good writer, I took a writing course. I looked at my skills in detail and did things to really shore myself up. Then once I was shored up—watch out. Then I was on a good solid fighting ground.

Anne proved herself time and again, worked her way up in her organization, and earned the respect of her managers and colleagues. She understood herself, leveraged her strengths, and took positive steps to improve on her areas of weakness. She didn't rely on others to tell her where she needed work, and she didn't rely on others to tell her she was great.

Be honest with yourself. Are you really better than the next person?

Blaming others for our inability to advance in the workplace is way too easy. There is plenty of evidence of ongoing discrimination and tactics against women, as presented in the previous and following chapters. But if you want to fight back, you need to make sure your qualifications and skills are up to snuff. You can't blame discrimination if someone else is clearly better than you at your job. That takes knowing yourself and knowing how others around you are performing.

As Anne says, "I've always been a fighter. But I also realized that sometimes you're not as good. It's a different situation. I really needed to find out for sure. Once I became sure, come hell or high water, I knew how to navigate."

It is important to understand both how you are doing and how (and what) your colleagues are doing. Even if you are excellent at your given task, if your colleague is showing leadership potential or working on areas that are more critical to the company's success, he or she may be considered more valuable. Pay close attention to what people talk about at meetings; sometimes this is the best way to understand what your management team values.

Try not to be discouraged when all you hear is the negative

If your company culture is to focus only on your areas of improvement, listen carefully to what they say, but don't take it too personally. I say this knowing full well I took it personally and it hurt me.

I went from companies where I got only glowing reviews of my awesomeness to a company whose performance evaluation forms allowed five bullet points for your strengths and five pages for your areas of improvement—literally. My first review I was stunned to hear so much negativity under the guise of "what could have gone better."

Each year, I felt like I was being punched in the gut while reading how I could have handled this or that situation better. I felt that way despite knowing that I had consistently exceeded my quota (I was in sales by then) and brought in an historic multimillion-dollar enterprise sale to a key organization in my territory.

Then I started to notice that my manager, who had written the review, had been in some of the meetings he was referring to where I "should have" said or done something different. He had not spoken up at the time or even afterward to coach me to change. It was as if the goal was to "catch" me doing something wrong, so he'd have things to say in the review. If the goal were truly to improve my performance or achieve a better result with the customer, he "should have" spoken up earlier, I thought.

In this environment, I found it very difficult to stay motivated and to improve, because I believed nothing would ever be good enough. I changed from an ambitious, driven employee to one whose mantra was, "The goal is to keep the job." I tried to follow their mandates for what they wanted me to do, realizing they would just keep raising the bar and finding fault no matter what I did.

Be honest: How easily do you give in to self-doubt?

Can you take criticism without falling apart? How do you react when someone tells you you've done something wrong? Do you take it personally, or can you separate your performance from your self-worth?

Studies have been conducted and many books written on how to deliver criticism to help others without damaging their egos. Unfortunately, most managers haven't read them, and some are better than others at delivering bad news.

Regardless of the method of delivery, we all have to learn to take advice and criticism in the spirit in which it is (or at least should be) intended: to improve our performance rather than tear us down.

I am the first to admit I've not always been good at that. In one case, when unfairly criticized in a peer quote in a performance evaluation, I became angry, argued the facts with my manager, and sent a rebuttal for my personnel file. I still stand by the truth, but I don't think my reaction helped me one bit. I was labeled as a troublemaker, put the person who wrote the unfair peer quote in a bad light (making our relationship awkward), and focused even more corporate attention on my areas that needed improvement.

As embarrassing as it is, I have also been brought to tears on occasion by a particularly cruel criticism. I hate myself for it during and after, but at the time could do nothing to stop it.

Fair or unfair, if you become offended and either lash out or cry, you will get labeled, and that will hurt you. We have all seen men become angry or upset at work, and they are either excused as "That's just Bill," or "He is so passionate about the truth." When a woman does it, she is told to "calm down" or is seen as weak and emotional.

Self-knowledge will keep you strong

The more you know your own strengths and weaknesses without waiting to be told, the more prepared you are when criticism comes your way.

If you already know where you need to improve and have figured out a plan for turning weaknesses around, you have a much better chance of keeping it together when you receive criticism. Instead of falling into self-doubt or anger, you can say, "Yes, I realize this, and here is what I am working on to strengthen in these areas." What a powerful response this would be!

It's not personal; it's business

Very few managers truly want to hurt you personally, and if they do, don't give them the pleasure of taking it that way. Generally speaking, criticism is meant to help you improve. The more you can keep this in mind, the less likely you are to react badly when confronted.

Nobody likes to make someone cry. Crying makes everyone uncomfortable. Even if the criticism is incredibly unfair or incorrect, crying takes away your power and credibility.

I am told that if you feel yourself beginning to cry, you can look up to stop the tears. I don't know if that works. I also recommend excusing yourself quickly, going to the bathroom or elsewhere to compose yourself, and then returning when you are feeling more confident. You can make a decision to table your emotions; then scream and cry later at home to get out your frustrations. Whatever it takes, whatever works for you, try to keep it together.

And if you don't succeed, quickly forgive yourself and find a way to reestablish your credibility and strength later. Our lives are a continuous learning process, and no one thing will completely derail us if we are determined.

What's the best way to motivate and evaluate employees?

Which is better: a performance evaluation system that focuses on your employees' strengths, one that focuses on their weaknesses, or a balanced approach? Or perhaps no formal system but rather a continuous coaching environment? Many studies have been conducted over the years, and new systems rolled out with the latest craze: 360-degree reviews, self-reviews, skip-level meetings, etc. In Silicon Valley, companies are starting to do away with the formal review process, realizing that the sheer cost of such systems makes it difficult to realize a return on the investment.

San Francisco-based rewards-and-recognition consulting firm Achievers in 2012 conducted a poll of 2,677 people (made up of 1,800 employees, 645 human resources managers, and 232 CEOs). "Although virtually all the companies surveyed use some form of annual evaluation as their chief means of giving performance feedback to employees, only 2% of HR people think these reviews accomplish anything useful."

Instead, employees prefer more real-time feedback. "While 61% of employees say they would welcome immediate, on-the spot feedback from bosses and peers about how they're doing, only 24% say they get it. "

In one study of 65,672 employees, Gallup found those who received strengths feedback had turnover rates that were 14.9% lower than for employees who received no feedback (controlling for job type and tenure).

General Electric (GE) eliminated the formal performance review in 2015 in favor of more immediate feedback with near-term goals and frequent discussions with managers on progress toward those goals.

Often we are given no choice about what type of performance evaluation process is required by the company. Regardless of the formal process, it is important to engage with your manager and employees on a regular basis—both to catch them doing something right and to correct in a timely manner when needed.

"Common sense" is not that common

When my daughter was very young, she used to play schoolhouse with her dolls and a few imaginary students in my sitting room. She was "Miss Keen" and had chalkboards and even an overhead projector and laminator. She gave elaborate lessons and encouraged her students to read and do their homework. When it was time for report cards, she would line her dolls up on the loveseat and lecture them. (I would listen from the other room, so she didn't know I was there.)

"Now students, I'm going to give you your report cards, but pay attention. If you got a good grade, that's great, but it's not an excuse to start slacking. You have to continue to work hard. If you got a bad grade, don't feel bad. It just means you have to start working harder and study more."

If we can all take Miss Keen's advice and use our performance evaluations to inspire us rather than discourage us, we will be doing well.

Even better, don't wait for your grade to know if you are doing well at your job. Assess your own strengths and weaknesses, judge your own improvements over time, and look around you to see how others are doing and what you need to do to keep up or exceed expectations.

Knowing your strengths, look for work and opportunities to capitalize on them. Knowing your weaknesses, find ways to bolster these areas. If you are self-aware and proactive in self-improvement, regardless of the review practices of your company or the criticism style of your managers, you empower yourself to advance.

CHAPTER 4

KNOW YOUR ENVIRONMENT AND OTHERS' MOTIVATIONS

CONSIDER AMY, a young, ambitious, recent Master of Business Administration (MBA) graduate who has just landed her first "adult" job with an up-and-coming company in her field. She is excited about the opportunity and ready to make her mark in the industry. Fresh out of her supportive, team-based graduate program, she is eager and full of ideas. She doesn't hesitate to speak up in meetings, put in the long hours necessary to complete projects, or take on extra assignments. Her boss, Mark, is happy to give her extra work and even gives her the added responsibility of keeping project notes and making sure there are adequate supplies and coffee for the team's long nights working on proposals. Amy is thrilled to be a part of it all.

While Amy is working late on a proposal, she notices Mark and some of the men on the team laughing together and cutting out early to go get beers. She shrugs it off—not really a beer drinker, and besides, she has a lot to do and can't afford to leave early. She and Allison make a fresh pot of coffee and talk about the next section. When they get to a point where they can't continue without Mark's input, they go home for the night, exhausted.

At the team meeting the next day, Amy makes a suggestion for a new approach to the final section of the proposal—one she had mentioned to John the day before. Mark gives a quick nod, then asks John to discuss his idea for the section they had talked about over beers the night before. John presents his case, which is not that different from Amy's approach. Mark smiles and says, "Great idea, John. Keep them coming, and you will go far." The men all smile and agree, and the meeting is concluded, leaving Amy sitting there wondering what just happened.

What did Amy miss? When she joined the company, she was eager about the work and didn't pay attention to the culture and dynamics of her department. When she agreed to take on extra work, she did it in the spirit of being a team player—and she didn't notice that she was given "busy work," while John and some others were given meatier roles. When she discussed her new idea with John casually in the lunchroom, she never considered that he would try to take credit for it. When the men all went out together, she considered it to be just a social thing she wasn't interested in rather than a continuation of business discussions and relationships.

Without a good understanding of the culture of the company, did Amy naively allow herself to be taken advantage of? In her eagerness to please and do the right thing for the company, did she accept assignments that put her in a support role rather than a path to advancement? Did the company have her best interests in mind?

What about John? Was he motivated to protect his own interests or those of the company rather than any notion of fairness and equality? What were his motivations for going out for beers with Mark and taking credit for Amy's idea?

How many of us have ignored or not noticed signs of an unsupportive company culture and have been hurt by it? How many of us—women and men—have been taken advantage of by a coworker or manager with less than charitable motivations?

Understand your organization and what drives people

Equally important as knowing your own strengths and areas for improvement is understanding your organization and the behavior and motivations of others around you. What is the corporate culture, and how does that affect how you are treated in comparison with others? Are women in general treated well, or do you see them being assigned less important roles or having their ideas dismissed? Are your coworkers and managers supportive and fair, or do they hold biases?

In this chapter, we will explore how the environment you work in can affect your ability to succeed—for better or worse. We will look at ways to recognize a negative culture and to negotiate within it or make the decision to leave. We will also look at how the behavior of others around us can affect you and what to do when others' motivations are hurting you or the company.

Leveraging your strengths in the context of how others around you behave will help you navigate the workplace with ease.

Corporate culture affects all levels

Don't expect smooth sailing until you get to the top. Discrimination can happen at any level, especially when the company culture is to value men over women in the same job.

Lisa noticed discrimination in her work environment even in an entry-level position. She was working for a company that provided a team to do inventory in stores around the country, busing them in for long hours of counting merchandise. After a few months, she realized her female manager, Joann, gave the men in the group immediate respect—placing them in more responsible jobs from the beginning. The women had to work hard to earn her respect—and often didn't get there. Lisa noticed the difference but was unsure how to handle it.

Was Joann simply conforming to a corporate culture of valuing men more than women, even though she was a woman herself? Was she trying to prove to her management that she wasn't going to coddle women just because she had been promoted? Or was it simply an unconscious reaction, a result of being raised in a male-dominated culture that respected men in the workplace more easily?

Whether what Lisa experienced was part of the larger culture of the company she worked for was unclear, because she was only exposed to her small work group. What was clear to Lisa was that she would have a hard time moving up in the organization with that particular manager who treated women unfairly. She ultimately left for another job, now more fully aware of how men and women can be treated differently in the work environment.

Promoting women based on past performance and men based on future potential

The tendency to promote men based on their potential, while requiring women to demonstrate their capabilities first, is not uncommon in the workplace. According to a 2011 McKinsey study, "The most insidious barriers for women are imbedded mindsets that halt their

58

KNOW YOUR ENVIRONMENT AND OTHERS' MOTIVATIONS

progress. . ... Several diversity officers and experts told us that despite their best efforts, women are often evaluated for promotions primarily on performance, while men are often promoted on potential."[1]

This phenomenon is perpetrated by women managers as well as men, at all levels of an organization, and may be unconscious or actually calculated. Of that we can't be sure. But the net effect is the same: men are advanced more quickly than women.

Once you figure it out, can you change it?

If Lisa had truly cared about this job, she might have challenged her manager's practices by asking for more responsible jobs or promoting her own capabilities. Sometimes it just takes a small effort to make someone realize they are acting unfairly. And sometimes it's a lot harder than that.

The more we challenge the assumptions that men are better at our jobs than we are—even if we aren't successful every time in changing minds or practices—the faster change will come. Unsettling a corporate culture that holds women back will help pave the way for others to succeed.

Believe in your own potential

The 2011 McKinsey study also found that many women "hold limiting beliefs that stand in their own way—such as waiting to fill in more skills or just waiting to be asked." Even Anne (in the previous chapter) acknowledged that she looked to herself first to be sure she had the skills she needed before fighting for a promotion. While it's important to be self-aware and to work to improve and develop the

---

1   Barsh, Joanna, and Lareina Lee. "Unlocking the Full Potential of Women at Work." McKinsey.com. http://www.mckinsey.com/client_service/organization/latest_thinking/unlocking_the_full_potential (accessed October 9, 2019).

needed experience and skills to move ahead, we also need to recognize that our *potential* can be as good or better than someone else wishing to move ahead.

Moreover, you can't change the mindset of an organization pitting men's potential against women's accomplishments if you don't believe in your own potential. Sometimes the only way to get the experience you need is to get the promotion or assignment before you have demonstrated you can do it. Don't let your own mindset get in the way.

Don't be afraid to speak up

Women Don't Ask: Negotiation and the Gender Divide, a book by Linda Babcock, highlights a disturbing trend shown in studies: women are not asking for raises or promotions nearly as often as men. They found that men initiate negotiations about four times as often as women. The cost to women for this tendency not to ask is huge: "Another study calculated that women who consistently negotiate their salary increases earn at least $1 million more during their careers than women who don't."

According to the authors, "Women tend to hesitate before asking for what they want not because of a silly blind spot that's entirely their own responsibility but because they are taught early on that pushing on their own behalf is unfeminine, unattractive, and unwelcome—not to mention ineffective." Note that a more recent study, *Women in the Workplace 2016* by LeanIn.org and McKinsey, found that "women negotiate for promotions and raises as often as men but face more pushback when they do. Not surprisingly, women are almost three times more likely than men to think their gender will make it harder to get a raise, promotion, or chance to get ahead."

Are you afraid to ask for what you want and deserve? Do you find yourself holding back from pressing for advancement? Are you afraid of being labelled as pushy or a complainer?

You are not alone, unfortunately. And based on Western society's cultural expectations, this is not an easy problem to fix. Fixing it starts with having confidence in your abilities and potential. Then you have to take the step forward. You have to *ask* to be considered for the promotion, *ask* for the raise—not in a pushy way but with confidence and respectful assertiveness. And if you receive pushback, don't give in too easily. Don't be a bargain.

Change can come from the top or from crisis

Lynn was first hired as a young engineer with the Navy around the time of the Tailhook scandal, a series of incidents in 1991 where U.S. Navy and Marine Corps officers were alleged to have sexually assaulted 83 women and seven men at a Tailhook Association symposium in Las Vegas. The resulting investigation revealed a culture within the military of hostility toward women, sexual harassment, and unequal treatment of women for career advancement. A number of officers were formally disciplined or refused advancements in rank, and policy changes were ultimately made to support women.

One would think that a young female engineer joining the Navy at this time would experience hostility, but because of the investigations and strict attention to this issue, Lynn found instead that she was treated very well. She and her friend Molly were the first female engineers in their part of the organization. Although all the positions above them were filled with men, they felt the Navy culture was "very healthy and productive," and Lynn and Molly felt their colleagues and officers watched out for them.

Who has your back?

Even when Lynn encountered awkward situations with colleagues, she was pleased to find her superiors pushing to change attitudes.

> Back when I first started out, I was the only female in a meeting. I had a shirt that had a button in the back, a shell. I noticed a guy was looking at me funny, and I said, "Can I help you with something?" He said "Yeah, I'm just trying to figure out how you get that shirt on." The commander couldn't believe it. He gave the guy a look and said, "If we're done with the non-value-added questions, can we get on with the meeting?" It was embarrassing to me.

Ultimately, though, the commander's reminder that this was inappropriate helped set the tone for the treatment of women in his organization. Lynn understood that she would be supported from the top, an important cultural shift.

Awareness of your environment is key

I have experienced many different cultures during my years of working as an engineer and in high-tech sales. In my first job after graduating, I felt simultaneously valued and undervalued. Under the guidance of my managers, I took on increasingly responsible positions as I demonstrated my capabilities. Within five years, I was program manager and systems engineer on a multimillion-dollar hardware and software project. I ignored other signs that the culture was not as supportive of women: blatant sexual harassment by some, no women in management, dismissive attitudes toward women's contributions, and crazy-making things like being told to "calm down" or asked to take notes in meetings. Only when I found out about the pay gap between Joey and me did I take a closer look at the culture and attitudes of my company. I fought for my rights—unsuccessfully, because the attitude of valuing men over women was so ingrained in my company. I had to leave the company for another job and come back a year later to a promotion and raise to correct some of that pay gap. I'll never know if it was completely fixed, because they kept Joey's salary hidden from me even when I was promoted above him.

Understanding the corporate culture can help you decipher the messages you are getting. Once I paid attention to the way women were treated at this company, I realized that equitable pay treatment would be difficult to achieve. I knew I would have to work harder, increase the visibility of my accomplishments, and continue to ask for fair treatment if I wanted to stay there.

Culture shock

If you are used to an environment where you have to fight for recognition and opportunity, you can be pleasantly surprised when you move to a company where women are valued and your talents are celebrated. When I left my last company, where the culture was extremely negative and oppressive, I felt devalued, down on myself, and sure I was a failure. I was thrilled to land a job in a smaller company where I feel supported, valued, and a huge contributor to the company's success. As a result of this positive attitude toward me, I am highly motivated and am at the top of the sales leader board. The CEO recently told me my former company was crazy to let me go, because I was "awesome." My VP of sales asked if I had a sister—wanting to hire another salesperson like me. (I really loved that he said "sister" and not "brother," especially in this male-dominated industry.)

Conversely, if you have grown used to a supportive environment, you can receive a real shock when you move to one that is less friendly toward women. When Lynn left her engineering job with the Navy to join a different government agency, she expected more of the same environment: a male-dominated culture seeking to change by nurturing women and providing growth opportunities. Instead, she found more of the old attitudes toward women and an expectation that she would follow the crowd.

As you move through your career, you will likely encounter both positive and negative attitudes toward the advancement of women in the workplace. The most successful women learn ways to negotiate all terrains.

Challenging a "yes person" culture

According to Lynn, her government agency has a group-think culture.

> If you don't act or think like them, you're an island. I was recently told, "From now on, don't clarify anything, express your opinion, elaborate on anything, or make conjectures, because they don't like that." Even though this is an engineering discussion. It's the culture. You are supposed to say, "Yes, I'm going to do it," even if you know you can't. You are not to talk about reality. What happens is someone like me—I come from shipbuilding and true systems engineering, so I understand the big picture— I can

see what's wrong. By speaking up, I get myself in
trouble.

In Lynn's view, this is not a male vs. female problem but an overall culture that inhibits creativity and progress for everyone. This
culture can exist in any organization, and it creates a problem for
both men and women. But in this environment, a strong, outspoken
woman like Lynn can feel stifled and vilified if she remains true to
herself. That hasn't stopped her.

"When I was younger and in a situation where some of the
women didn't like me because I didn't act like them, I asked one of
the guys what to do. He said, 'Lynn, just be who you are. Don't forget
who you are. Don't start acting like the people you think you need
to act like. Be who you are and if you are honest about that, you'll
be fine.'"

Lynn has carried that advice through many difficult situations,
developing savvy to work successfully within different environments. She watches and learns from the culture of the organization
and the behavior of the people within it. With full confidence in
doing the right thing, she continues to challenge and put forth her
ideas to effect positive change.

Individual motivations—borne of the culture or something else?

Sometimes we are puzzled by the behavior of our coworkers or
managers and find it difficult to understand their motivations. By
first understanding the context—the corporate culture—we can
sometimes find the answers. But there are many contributing causes
to how someone acts in a given situation, from trouble at home to
ingrained sexism to poor work ethic to just having a bad day. Really

getting to know the people around us and what motivates them can help us negotiate with integrity and grace.

Doesn't everyone want to do their best and make the company succeed?

In a word, no. You have to assume that others may not have the best motivations toward the job for their own reasons. Consider a man—let's call him John—who hates his job, hates coming to work, and just wants to put in his eight hours and go home. He may do the minimum work he can get away with while daydreaming about what he will do that weekend. Then imagine you come in, full of fire and motivation and great ideas for innovative new things. John immediately resents you, because you are going to make him look bad, and probably your ideas are going to make him have to work harder. It shouldn't be surprising to find him bashing your ideas in meetings or behind your back, even if they would be great for the company.

This can be witnessed with both men and women. Lynn has seen it among her colleagues, in particular with a woman who is not very competent but is in a senior position:

> Her favorite color is green, and everyone knows it. If you're a woman, you wear green, and you're subservient—say "Yes, yes"—and admire her. Then she'll help you. If you are competent but don't do that, she won't help you. She's says she's a very staunch feminist, but she does that and doesn't help women. It's very contrary behavior, very narcissistic, because, if you are competent and not like that, and you are compared with her, she looks bad.

Each person around you has the potential to help you or hurt you. The more you understand whom you are dealing with, the better you will be able to ward off threats and find those who will help you.

How can someone not like me?

Years ago, I joined a very small company as an applications engineer and quickly became director of sales and marketing. The company had female engineers but no women in management positions aside from the boss's wife, who was the chief financial officer (CFO). In my new role, I needed the support of various women in the operations group for quotes, invoicing, and customer service. I was always very polite when requesting their help and thanked them every time for whatever they did for me. In general, I'm a friendly, upbeat person who practices kindness in the workplace. In my prior jobs, I was well liked.

That's why I was completely surprised that the women in this company didn't like me. I overheard them making snarky comments about me behind my back, and I often got passive-aggressive behavior from them. Deanna would say, "Sure, I'll take care of that for you," then set it aside and never look at it again—hurting me and the company in the process. Even the CFO, who was friends with the other women in the office, took to bad-mouthing me in meetings for reasons I'll never understand. (I tripled sales in the first year, so it was more likely jealousy than any concerns with my performance.)

Without knowing for sure, I came to believe they didn't like taking "orders" from a woman. I was more educated, harder-working, and in a higher position. I had created and filled a new position within the company and changed things to improve sales. Was I a threat to their status quo or to their egos? Regardless of their reasons, their actions made for an awkward working environment.

The hardest part for me was not taking it personally, because at first I found it very hurtful. I consulted with former colleagues, who were surprised that anyone wouldn't like me. I had to make a conscious decision to let it go, stay professional, and consider this as business and not personal. I stuck to my guns, documented my requests and their responses in case anything got dropped, and tried to remain consistently upbeat and appreciative of their efforts.

Please note: When you rely on others to do work for you, you have to find a way to make that work. Some people respond to kindness, others are self-motivated, and still others may need a direct exploration of the issue.

What if someone's attitude is hurting me or the company?

We have all run across the "negative Nellies"—people who can never be happy, complain about everything, shoot down all ideas, and contribute nothing positive to a conversation. Getting drawn into negativity is all too easy, as we will explore in a later chapter. Simply put: don't go there.

It's not always clear why someone has a bad attitude; the reason could be something completely unrelated to work or just a bad day. But what if their behavior is keeping you from getting your work done or actually hurting the company? Depending on your position relative to the person causing the problems, you may have to either address it directly or get management or Human Resources involved, as difficult as these options may be. Letting it slide indefinitely could hurt your own career.

How do I escape feeling that I am always in competition?

First, accept that you are always in competition. Your performance is being judged in the workplace; it's as simple as that. That is how you get raises, promotions, and other recognition. Other people want the higher positions and raises just as you do.

Competition can be healthy and usually is. If nobody around you is motivated to do good work, it's hard to care enough to do your very best. If others are working hard and showing initiative, that should be motivating to you to do the same. Even if you are in a laid-back environment that seems non-competitive, you need to bring your best to work every day. You can be the example that others follow.

Do YOUR best, document, and self-promote

Obviously, you should put forth your best efforts at work if you want to succeed and move ahead. But doing excellent work is insufficient if nobody knows about it. As difficult as you may find it to toot your own horn, make sure you are given credit for what you have achieved—that's critical.

This can be done in many ways, both subtle and more obvious. If a customer or colleague is especially thankful to you for something you have done, ask them to send a note to your manager, or forward any notes they have sent you. This may seem bold, but I have had many customers happy to do that, and it helps management to know how well I am doing.

A quick email to the boss telling him about a project you just completed is sometimes enough to make sure he is aware. Trip reports and other formal reports can sometimes be useful to spread the word about a new initiative you are working on. An email follow-up from a meeting can remind attendees of new ideas you put forth, especially if you fear someone else is taking credit for your idea. Even a short, casual conversation with a manager or executive about a project you are working on can raise awareness. The more people within the organization that know who you are and what you are accomplishing, the easier it will be to get raises and promotions approved.

Documenting your work is also a very good way to protect against anyone's trying to take credit for what you have done. It can also maintain a valuable record of how a project progressed, how and why decisions were made, and when changes in direction occurred. This can be quite helpful when explaining a situation to management or when a new person joins the team and wants to understand the reasoning behind decisions.

How do you counter trash-talking?

One of the tactics used against women—or anyone—in the workplace is to talk badly about them. Sometimes you will know what is being said, and sometimes you won't. Lynn has seen plenty of it:

> I'm in some of the discussions. What they do, I know that they are looking for someone, and that what is most important is that someone can write well. So they will say, "I just love Sue; she's so great; she just can't write—such a good person." The little thing that was said—"she can't write"—why would

you hire her, if that's the most important thing to you? I've seen several character assassinations done smiling and friendly, but if they point out the one thing that is important ('she can't write'), they have killed that person.

Lynn has heard it about herself:

> A woman that I had some issues with got promoted. She put in my package that I had trouble with communication and relating to people. Someone came up to me and asked, "Why aren't you up for this job. Your name didn't get put in?" I said, "I did put my name in, but I didn't get called up. What's going on? Obviously something I'm not doing—help me figure it out." Rumor was that I couldn't effectively communicate. They have me doing the work and someone else getting the glory at the end. I don't get it. They keep telling people I'm invaluable but then don't recommend me for promotion. I'm stuck. They want me to stay and do the work and let them get the recognition. They have promoted these people that can't do the work and created deputy positions, and now they want me to go shore them up.

As difficult as it is to hear the bad things said about you, you are much better off knowing than not knowing. You may not be able to directly respond, especially if they are said outside your presence. But you can then use that as fuel to demonstrate your capabilities and make sure there is plenty of evidence to the contrary.

Even while this reputation for poor communication is out there, a colleague tells Lynn, "I watch you and try to learn from you in meetings, because you handle everybody so well—that right mix of letting everybody speak." The idea of her not being able to communicate is ludicrous. By maintaining her integrity and continuing to do good work, the truth eventually comes out.

Track your progress

Keep a "brag folder" in your desk or computer with notes about things you have done well through the year, including any positive feedback you have received from anyone. I always have a separate email folder with any positive feedback emails in it, as well as folders on my computer and a physical file as needed. This will come in very handy if you need to do a self-review at the end of the year or if you want to provide input or rebuttal to a manager's review. I have found this useful for keeping track of my progress through the years with a company and critical when putting together my self-review. It can also help you keep your resume up to date, which is always a good idea even if you have no intention of leaving your job.

One of the side benefits of having a brag folder and an up-to-date resume is to remind yourself on a regular basis what you have accomplished and the progress you have made. Especially on difficult days, this can provide a much-needed ego boost.

If you decide to leave your company, be sure to bring your brag folder with you. It will be a valuable resource for you as you update your resume and helpful to review before interviews, so you are up to date and confident in your strengths and accomplishments. I always find myself more prepared and confident when interviewing for a new job or a promotion if I have taken the time to refresh my memory on specific successes I have had through the years.

Watch what others are doing

Doing your job well is one thing, but understanding how that fits within the larger organization and how what you are doing compares with what others are doing, is another. If you see others getting choice assignments, extra training, or more face time with upper management, take note. They may be getting special treatment that will fast track them for promotion. If you want to keep up, you will need to put yourself out there and ask for similar opportunities. Don't wait until it's too late to speak up.

In Lynn's current environment, the favoritism and discrimination are rampant. She sees her colleagues being sent for important training and being put up for promotions she is denied because she is not one of the favorites. While Lynn is working hard and getting things done, these colleagues are going to luncheons, conferences, and trainings. "I've been watching them. It starts to affect your motivation, and effectiveness, and it's hard not to feel resentful. I had five specific requests for my attendance, but I had never heard about them, because they were refusing to let me go." However, Lynn finds it more important to maintain her integrity by not kowtowing to the narcissistic manager, so she continues to put forth new ideas and do the hard work. Other colleagues and managers recognize her value and are now pushing to have her put in for training and promotions previously denied her. She is also taking the time to attend important conferences and enjoying well-earned vacations. "I had to learn how to respond to their behavior but not become them."

If you notice a colleague has especially good presentation skills, and you know this is an area you need to improve on, take steps to bring your skill level up. Ask for more opportunities to practice, take a public speaking course either through your work or on your own, or join Toastmasters. Take responsibility to ensure your skills will get you where you want to go.

Finding the win-win that allows you to achieve success in an unfair world

We all want to find the win-win, the one idea that will let both my opponent and me succeed. In many situations, win-win doesn't exist. A football game is won by one team and lost by another—even a tie is not considered a win-win.

But wherever possible, strive to find ways to negotiate even the most unfair business environments to move up without dragging someone else down. While every situation is different, a key element to doing this is to maintain your integrity and respect for others. Lynn's view is this:

> There are different types of people. Those with competence but no integrity and those with integrity but no competence often are moved into positions of power, and they are threatened by people with both. People with integrity and competence either shut down, are vocal—career suicide, or become one of them. But for me and some others, instead we are aware of the environment, and keep on keeping on. Every day we put in our 110%, are able to look at ourselves in the mirror, and just hope not to see these people.

Even in the most competitive situations, where one person is clearly the winner, maintain your integrity and grace. Being a poor winner is even worse than being a poor loser. Where possible, find ways to recognize the accomplishments of the other side or at least allow them to save face. This will serve you well in your career, as well as your life.

How do I find a strategy to get ahead?

Every situation is different, and there are multiple ways to navigate any career path. This yields two key points: there is no one-size-fits-all strategy, and no matter what path you take, you can still achieve success.

When choosing a strategy to move forward in a given situation, you must fully understand your environment—the culture of your company and your work group. You must also understand the specific people around you who will impact or be affected by your decisions. Pay attention to the trends in your workplace and the behavior of those around you. Listen to how others talk about you or about women in general. See what is working for other women and men in your career field. Get to know your managers and coworkers so you understand their motivations.

One great way to learn more about the goals of the company is to read the mission statement and any other information available on the company website or internal network. If something is unclear to you, reach out to management and ask questions—they will be impressed that you made the effort to understand the corporate goals. Tie your personal goals into the corporate goals, if possible.

In company social situations, try to talk with someone new each time and learn about what they do and what they enjoy. You don't have to work the room like a pro—just make connections a little at a time. The more you know, the better decisions you will make.

And if you find yourself in an environment that stifles you, or you feel you have made a wrong turn on your career path, do not despair. Sensible women learn from all their experiences and choose better paths based on this hard-earned knowledge. And, as you will learn in the next chapter, they know when to ask for guidance and help.

CHAPTER 5

SEEK HELP
FROM OTHERS

NOW YOU KNOW HOW to recognize when you have become a threat, what tactics might be used against you, and how to assess and improve on your own strengths and weaknesses. You have studied the company culture to better understand its trends, and you have studied those around you to better understand their motivations.

Sometimes what you will discover will feel like a field full of landmines. How do you learn to negotiate it without getting blown up? You get help.

But I'm smart. Why do I need help?

Being determined doesn't mean you know how to move within your company or organization. Promotions are often based on who you know and spend time with both inside and outside the organization, and women can be excluded from the informal boys' clubs that still exist today.

Jane, a recent computer science graduate, was only at her new company a couple of months when she realized she was being treated differently from her male colleagues. At her first meeting, she was asked to take notes and was told they would take turns in this role in the future. At first, she didn't mind, because she found it useful to capture everything going on and review it later before sending the notes to the group. As she became more familiar with the project, she had more of her own ideas to put forth and found the note-taking a distraction from the content of the meeting. Once she realized she had taken notes at 30 meetings in a row, she decided to ask for help. She emailed her manager, "It has been a good learning experience taking notes for the meetings since I first joined. Now that I have had that task for the past 30 meetings, I think the project could benefit from a new perspective. Could we go back to the round robin approach of having the team members take turns in this role?"

Was this really asking for help? Yes. She could have just kept doing what was asked of her without question, something women do all too often to keep from making waves. Or she could have complained to her teammates that she was the only one taking notes and it wasn't fair—another common mistake that could have had her labeled as negative and likely wouldn't have resulted in changed behavior. Instead, she confronted it directly, with a positive spin, and asked her manager to facilitate the change.

Exposing unfairness

Jane's asking her manager to correct an unfair situation also served as a statement: *I want to be treated the same as the men on the team.*

She had noticed biases and inappropriate comments by her senior manager and was concerned about how that would affect her ability to move ahead. He had recently said to her and her female manager, "I just love being able to say *'the girls'* when I refer to your team. We've never had an all-girl team before." He also told Jane that her predecessor was "just this little girl, but it turns out she really knew stuff."

Since Jane is a petite young woman, she found it hard not to take offense at this comment. Why would a young woman with a computer science degree *not* be expected to "know stuff"? Being referred to as a "girl" in the workplace can be very damaging, as it does not command the same respect as being called a "woman." Somehow the impression is that you are a child with child-like sensibilities and intelligence. You never hear men being called "boys" in the workplace.

As an affirmation of the senior manager's bias, he recently told Jane and her manager, "I call the computer 'she,' because she is so temperamental."

It is difficult to know how to respond in these situations. How do you tell the senior manager he is being an ass? How do you get away from being called a "girl" by your coworkers and managers?

Jane came to me asking for advice. She knows it is difficult to change your senior manager, so she has to find a way to work within the system, if she can. She will be up for a promotion next year, and she wants to make sure she has a fair shot at it.

Jane's understanding of her environment and recognition of the challenges ahead will help guide her actions and know what behaviors to avoid. She knows the senior manager is likely sexist, and she needs to be aware of how that affects the culture she is working in. Within that framework, she can push back against bias when she sees it, as she did with the issue of taking notes at meetings. She should stop referring to her other female colleagues as "girls," as I found her doing as she explained the situation to me. It may seem strange to talk about your former college classmates as women, but the sooner you give up childhood references in the workplace, the sooner you can be taken seriously. And, as I advise all women, assess your strengths, watch what others are doing around you, self-promote, volunteer for the hard stuff, and get help when you need it.

IT's a "man's world"

Just a couple of years out of college, Jane encounters sexism as a computer programmer in that still-male-dominated field. Valerie started in IT back in the '70s, when it was a relatively new field, and women programmers were practically non-existent. In addition to being demoted because she wouldn't sleep with her boss, she was told, "Oh, you're a girl, and we've been told we have to hire a girl. So you just be the token girl and don't worry about it."

There was no one for Valerie to ask how to deal with these issues. There were neither women in management nor peers for her to ask, and she was afraid to alienate the men she was working with and for by complaining about sexism.

But she was raised by a strong woman who ran a farm and raised five kids after Valerie's father died when Valerie was five years old.

> Watching Mom work hard, in a man's world, too, I didn't recognize it back then. She ran the farm, in-teracted with men—did what she had to do. Always emphasized "Work hard, study hard, don't depend on other people to make decisions and do things for you, and be able to take care of yourself, because you never know what's going to happen in life." She didn't know she'd be left with a farm and kids to

SEEK HELP FROM OTHERS

raise. What she taught me is the backbone of what I
am and what I do.

Valerie kept her head focused on her personal career goals,
dodged sexual advances as needed, and worked harder than anyone
else. "As a programmer, you can sit at your desk and program and
prove yourself. There were times when I felt like I worked harder
than my male counterparts to prove I could do it. There was a lot
of that. Still is. There were times I worked all night long to fix a
problem when they went home at 8 p.m.—or I volunteered to fix a
problem to prove that I could. In fact, I had to prove myself every
step of the way."

But don't we all have to prove ourselves?

Yes, men also have to prove they can do the work. Very few people
can succeed without showing they are capable and effective. Coming
in with credentials—degree, experience, references, etc.—helps,
but it is only the start. Your day-to-day performance is what truly
counts.

Valerie believes that she had to work harder than the men
around her to get what she wanted: increased salary and recognition
and promotions. And she is not alone: all the women I interviewed
said they had to work harder than men to achieve success. Various
studies support this theory, including a 2015 Harvard Law survey[2]
of Harvard Law graduates showing that female lawyers worked
longer hours for lower pay than the male graduates.

2   Wilkins, David B., Byron Fong, and Ronit Dinovitzer. "The Women and Men of
    Harvard Law School: Preliminary Results from the HLS Career Study." Harvard Law
    School, Center on Legal Profession. https://clp.law.harvard.edu/assets/HLS-Career-
    Study-FINAL.pdf (accessed October 14, 2019).

This may not be true in all occupations and all companies, of course. But given the obstacles women face in the workplace, it is incumbent on us to put our best selves forward. Men certainly need to prove themselves to move ahead, but they are less likely to become a threat to the status quo—or to someone's ego—by trying to move up.

The more we understand about how to move past the obstacles, the more we will succeed. And sometimes, that means working harder than our male colleagues.

Eventually, Valerie's manager was unable to deny her the promotions she clearly earned. But that doesn't take her off the hook:

> Even now, I know my boss is going to retire next year and that I'm slated for his position, but I still feel like if there's an opportunity to put myself out there and give presentations in front of customers and clients, I volunteer. I'll give that presentation; I'll do that research on the cloud—to prove myself, build credibility. Once the CIO [chief information officer] position comes open, I want my name out there so that when he retires, people will think, "Oh, obviously Valerie's going to take that." Men probably also do that but don't feel the same way about it. They probably look at it as getting their name out there. That's valid. I feel that, but I feel a stronger need for people to know I worked for it, I know how to do this, and I'm not a token. I know cloud computing, and the future of where it will go. I know this. All the CIOs I work with are all men. All our customers are men. I have to prove I can do my job as well as any of them.

In high school, it's cliques. In executive circles, it's the "boys' club."

Valerie kept her head down, worked hard, and got her promotions. Now that she has reached the executive level, she is seeing new challenges to negotiate. These become especially apparent when they are on executive retreats and conferences.

> Now as an executive, it's a whole new thing. There's a good old boys' club, and the wives of the good old boys. They've been executives for years and have this male bonding thing going on. I don't fit in with the wives but am not one of the good old boys either. I go to meetings and do my job; then they go play golf and whatever they want to do. I do my thing socially separate from them. I just do my job, give my presentations, run the show, do whatever I need to do; then I just go off by myself or with other executive women in the same boat. We're not going to hang out with the wives and not going to play golf. What are we going to do? It's awkward. This happens in a lot of corporations, not just where I work; this is the case at the executive level.

Deciding where you fit in a situation like this can be tricky. I have run into this on business trips with male colleagues when they all want to go for beers, I would be the only female if I joined, and it's clear they would prefer to just "hang with the guys." Men who aren't athletic or interested in golf or don't want to go drinking probably also have trouble fitting in. Is this just a social problem, or does it affect business?

I asked Valerie, "How does this affect you now as far as promotability, recognition, salary?"

> I think it does affect that. I'm not sure, because I don't know what I don't know—because I'm not in the good old boys' club. I see women trying to figure that out. Other women execs try to play golf or go out drinking with the guys. I don't think that works any better. I think the men look at each other and think they are making everything happen, are superior, and therefore deserve the bigger salary—because they've gotten together and patted each other on the back and told each other how wonderful they were. I think they get bigger bonuses and salaries because of that. They justify it.

Placing a value on business relationships and what goes on outside the office is difficult. Many women have struggled with how much to join in with their male colleagues on outings. Retaining a professional image and reputation is important for women, and mixing it up with the boys over beers could lead to even more awkward situations than being left out.

Still, the fact is, business is discussed outside the office, sometimes decisions are made, and if you are not there, you are not a part of the decisions. This is also where trust and bonding is developed through common experiences. As a result, you need to figure out the best way to interact with your colleagues and managers in all situations, and sometimes that requires asking for help. A senior manager who is more "in the know" about the social and political dynamics in your office may be able to provide specific guidance.

How do you know when to ask?

Asking for help can come in many forms. Sometimes it is as simple as asking a coworker to assist with a difficult assignment or asking to be put in a training class in an area in which you would like to improve. For more complex situations, such as gender discrimination or sexual harassment, a careful approach is recommended. More information on the laws to protect you and how to handle these situations can be found in Chapter 6.

Generally speaking, any time you find yourself struggling with a problem, consider whether there is an opportunity to get help. Often women feel they need to tough it out and do all the work themselves to prove they can do it. This can be a mistake. Seeking help—whether it's asking the advice of a colleague with more experience in your area, asking your manager how to handle a situation, or asking Human Resources for advice on a tricky personnel issue—is a sign of strength, not weakness. The more quickly you can solve a problem, the better.

Even if you are not currently encountering trouble, you may benefit from finding a mentor to guide you through your career path. Often a mentor can give you strategies for getting visibility or training you may need.

Asking for help can be an art

Valerie worked her way up to vice president of information technology at a large insurance company. She didn't get there by doing everything herself. Getting others to help her—whether colleagues, direct reports, or CEO—is critical to her success. This means she gives direct taskings to men and women, not all of whom are completely comfortable with taking orders from a woman. With her

Southern charm, firm but easygoing manner, sense of humor, and good old-fashioned ego-stroking, Valerie has made giving taskings an art form:

> I get along well with the guys. Mine are okay with me giving them direction. No problems. They respect me, know if they come to me they will get a straight answer—not emotional. I give direction based on facts, not emotion. It's the right thing to do. They know I'll listen to them; they just come in to do their job. They don't have a problem with me.
>
> Some women managers do have problems with men or other women who don't like to take direction from women. I have to say all the men that work for me I hired. I wouldn't have hired someone that couldn't take direction from me."

Valerie is fortunate to have a hand-picked staff who respect her. They also know she is there to help them and not take advantage of them for her own gain—which makes them more willing to accept direction from her. But she has also cultivated ways to get others to agree to do things for her.

"Men are easy"

One way Valerie manages her people is to know what makes each of them tick, what motivates them, and what they need from her as a manager. According to Valerie:

> Men are easy. If you find their ego spot, it's easy and so subtle. Nobody even recognizes it. Just simple things like, "I know you're the expert on this, and

I know you can help me," "You're the only one who ever comes to my aid on this; you always fix this," "Your direction is always so spot on," "Could you have a meeting, because I have some really important people who want to hear what you have to say," or "I know you're gonna do a presentation at the president's banquet, because you have so many good things to say, and you do such awesome work."

This sounds manipulative, right? If she were lying to get her way, it definitely would be. But everything she says is true, and she knows that her employees want to be appreciated. Her approach is based on basic kindness. Her comments must be sincere and not overdone. The better she knows who she is working with, the more tailored her feedback is to meet their specific needs. She uses this technique with peers, her direct reports, and even those above her in the corporation:

One is a programmer on the floor. Nobody likes him, because he's gruff and says what he wants to say. I'll call him up and say, "Tom, I need you to fix this problem." He'll start complaining, "Why? It's not my problem. Somebody else created it," and I'll say "I know, I know, but I need you to do this for me." "Oh, okay. Well, the boss wants me to do it." He needs that little stroking. I have people come to me saying, "We need Tom to fix this," but he won't do it for them. "He's just a jerk. If you call him, he'll do it." "Okay, I'll call and tell him to do it." Within an hour, he'll have it done.

Our architect's ego you couldn't fit in the house, but I can call him and say, "You are always just so brilliant on this stuff, I need you to help me." Works every time.

With executives like the president, it's 'Well, you know, you do this, because you're really important, and you need to be out there. You know you're good at it; you need to just shine." Oh, that just strokes his ego.

Valerie has figured out what each person needs, so she can tailor her requests for the best results. Her goals are to motivate people to do the job, to reward them for doing well, and to give them incentive to continue to help her. You could call it manipulative, but it's just good people skills. The more managers understand what motivates their staff, the more successful they will be. And most people are motivated by praise and positive feedback. I know I am.

Note that Valerie is not asking for outlandish things or for people to help her to the detriment of the company. Because she is honest, hardworking, effective, and kind, her colleagues like and respect her. People trust that what she is saying is true, even the ego-stroking, and they appreciate feedback from someone they respect.

Women need a different approach

Valerie doesn't use the ego-stroking with women—or at least not in the same way. She finds women just want to get their work done and be appreciated. So she does more commiserating. She will say to one of the female executives she works with, "I know you get all the crap stuff, so I'll help you."

Valerie has found that the women she works with want something different:

> Women want to know their work is recognized. I
> will say to them, "I know you are working hard,
> and you have a lot on your plate. Can you do this
> one other thing?," or "I know you've got a lot of
> problems going on right now, so let us help you with
> this," or "I really appreciated your helping me do
> this this and this. You took time out of everything
> you had on your plate to help me, and I wanted you
> to know I appreciated that." It's just different, more
> professional and more even. Just recognize every-
> thing they are doing, what they are working on.
> If you give women (or men) recognition, they will
> bend over backwards to help you.

I have found this to be true in my work as well. I am by nature an appreciative person, and I always make sure to recognize the efforts of those who help me—both privately and publicly. Then the next time I need something, there are no issues. I also know myself, and I am much more motivated to help someone who recognizes my achievements and appreciates my efforts. This is human nature.

Humor can take away the sting

According to Valerie, "I was being bossy one day to some guy. 'I want you to do this and this and this.' It was one of those days when things were crazy, and I didn't have time for a 30-minute conversation using soft skills. It was just 'Do this, this, this,' and he said, 'You sound like my wife.'"

YOU HAVE WHAT IT TAKES

Ouch. Valerie's first thought was, *Do NOT compare me to your wife. This will not go well for either of us.* But she bit her tongue and decided to use humor instead.

"Fine, if you want to be like that," she responded with a wicked smile and shaking her finger at him. "You just sit down and listen to me and do what I tell you, or you are in big trouble, Mister." They shared a laugh, and the man got right to work on her requests.

You can't lead if nobody is following

Respect breeds respect. If you treat your colleagues, managers, and those below you with respect, you will receive it in return. People want to help people they like and respect, especially those who are appreciative of their efforts. This is not rocket science.

Conversely, if you create a hostile environment, you will be surrounded with hostility. Nobody wants to work like that. Hostility can also get you fired.

Mentors and sponsors

In addition to needing help with day-to-day responsibilities and problems, many women can benefit from more formal coaching, either within or outside their organizations. Some organizations now have internal mentoring programs in which more senior staff advise mentees on career advancement. Even if your company doesn't have such a program, you can ask someone you admire if they would be willing to coach you on occasion. This can be just a lunch once a month or once a quarter to discuss what is going on in the company, how you are progressing, how you feel about your advancement possibilities, etc. The mentor can advise you on how to work with a specific manager or increase your visibility in the company. Their inside knowledge can be very helpful.

If you are very lucky, that person can be more of a sponsor—someone who will help you move up in the organization by promoting your abilities and helping you break down barriers. For fear of showing favoritism, some executives would find it difficult to mentor or sponsor someone in their organization. However, many of these same people would be willing to serve as a mentor for women outside their company.

Finding a mentor or sponsor

Connecting with a mentor or sponsor who is willing to help you in your career can be challenging but very rewarding. Here's how to do it effectively:

1. Know what you are looking for. Take time to evaluate your goals and how a mentor or sponsor can help you.

    » Career guidance from someone who has walked the path you are striving for?

    » Someone to run ideas/issues by to get advice?

    » A sponsor to help you navigate the internal politics of your organization and to promote your abilities to others? (This should be someone working for your company.)

    » Someone to challenge you to improve?

    » Someone to whine to about how hard it is? (In this case, get a therapist or talk to your friends or spouse. This is not the job of a mentor.)

2. Be involved and be known. Get to know people who can help you. Networking, even if you hate it, is critical to finding the right mentor.

» At company functions, make a goal to sit next to someone new and get to know them. If you always sit and talk with the same coworkers, you are missing an opportunity to learn.

» Join industry groups and play an active part. Volunteer for organizing events, run for office, work the signup desk, or take whatever role makes sense for you to get to know the members and key players in your industry.

» Give talks. Be part of a panel discussion. Pay attention to who the movers and shakers are. At industry trade shows, make a goal to sit with key players at lunch, introduce yourself, and learn more about them.

3. Ask someone you know or are getting to know for a brief meeting or for coffee. Have a specific agenda or advice you are seeking—something small, perhaps—to see how well you click, how willing they are to help, and how useful their advice is. Feel them out on whether they would be interested in being a mentor for you. You may do this with several people before you find a good fit.

4. Ask the person to be your mentor.

» Set expectations properly: how many meetings you anticipate, what type of advice you are looking for, etc.

» Be respectful of their time and be sure to honor any commitments you make.

» Being a good mentee means listening, giving fair consideration of the advice offered, acting on the suggestions where they make sense, and showing appreciation for the mentor's time and advice.

Helping each other

Valerie is interested in helping women avoid some of the obstacles she encountered when coming up through the ranks in IT. She regularly advises women who work for her but would not feel comfortable serving as a formal mentor or sponsor for anyone in her company. She is looking into outside organizations where she can help.

"I'd like to help other women navigate these waters, because I feel like I've blazed a trail. Especially in IT, hopefully we've made it better for the next generation. I don't know if we have or not, or if we've just been stubborn and have gotten through it—got ourselves through it, not made it better for other people." Her advice is sprinkled throughout the chapters in this book, for starters.

CHAPTER 6

KNOW THE LAW AND HOW TO USE IT

THERE ARE LAWS against discrimination, and they have been around for many years. However, even with today's increased awareness of the law, violations occur all the time. In some cases, there is a perception that women will either not notice the discrimination or won't want to make waves, so employers can get away with it. The higher a woman rises in the ranks, the more likely it is that she will run into this.

Women need to know what protections are in place, pay attention to what is happening to them and around them, and be prepared to call foul when necessary. The more we bring attention to unfair practices, the easier it will be to change them.

First, you must know where you stand vis-à-vis your rights in the workplace.

What are my rights?

There are many laws in the United States protecting various aspects of women's rights. Here is a quick summary of a few of them, from the Equal Employment Opportunity Commission website (eeoc.gov):

Title VII of the Civil Rights Act of 1964 (Title VII): This law makes it illegal to discriminate against someone on the basis of race, color, religion, national origin, or sex. The law also makes it illegal to retaliate against a person because the person complained about discrimination, filed a charge of discrimination, or participated in an employment discrimination investigation or lawsuit. The law also requires that employers reasonably accommodate applicants' and employees' sincerely held religious practices unless doing so would impose an undue hardship on the operation of the employer's business.

The Pregnancy Discrimination Act: This law amended Title VII to make it illegal to discriminate against a woman because of pregnancy, childbirth, or a medical condition related to pregnancy or childbirth. The law also makes it illegal to retaliate against a person because the person complained about discrimination, filed a charge of discrimination, or participated in an employment discrimination investigation or lawsuit.

The Equal Pay Act of 1963 (EPA): This law makes it illegal to pay different wages to men and women if they perform equal work in the same workplace. The law also makes it illegal to retaliate against a person because the person complained about discrimination, filed a charge of discrimination, or participated in an employment discrimination investigation or lawsuit.

The Age Discrimination in Employment Act of 1967 (ADEA): This law protects people who are 40 or older from discrimination because of age. The law also makes it illegal to retaliate against a person because the person complained about discrimination, filed a charge of discrimination, or participated in an employment discrimination investigation or lawsuit.

I've included that last one to point out that there are all kinds of reasons people are discriminated against, and sometimes sorting through the *why* is less important than realizing you are not being treated fairly. Regardless of the reasons, we need to learn to recognize discrimination so we can learn to defend and protect ourselves. The fact is, the law forbids discrimination when it comes to any aspect of employment, including hiring, firing, pay, job assignments, promotions, layoff, training, fringe benefits, and any other term or condition of employment.

But what is discrimination?

According to the *Merriam-Webster Dictionary*, discrimination is the practice of unfairly treating a person or group of people differently from other people or groups of people. If you see that men are getting opportunities for advancement or special treatment in comparison to how women are treated in your workplace, you could be witnessing gender discrimination. If you notice there are many fewer women than men in management, you may question why that is and see whether gender discrimination has contributed to this. If you discover you are making less money than a male colleague with less experience or education than you, you may be a victim of discrimination. If you find yourself passed up for promotion because you are pregnant or have children at home, you may be a victim of discrimination.

In spite of the laws to protect us, gender discrimination still exists. I have experienced all of these examples, and the women whose stories appear in this book have experienced or seen many more.

What is not discrimination?

When you are one of the only females in a male-centric environment, you might be tempted to label any challenges to your performance as discrimination. Be very careful—not just for your sake but also for the sake of those women with real discrimination cases. As we discussed in Chapter Three, you need to know your own strengths and weaknesses, as well as recognize when you need to improve in an area. As Anne did any time she felt someone else was getting ahead, look first to yourself to make sure you are not lacking in some area that is important. If you have done a true self-assessment, and you believe you are more qualified than the other person, then you may be experiencing discrimination. Getting the opinion of a trusted colleague who might provide a more objective view of the situation can be helpful.

You may also want to examine your work environment as a whole: Are women treated with respect? Do you frequently hear sarcastic comments about women or witness sexual harassment? Sex discrimination often flourishes in work environments where sexual harassment is permitted or ignored.

What about sexual harassment?

The Equal Employment Opportunity Commission website (eeoc. gov) also summarizes the laws on harassment:

It is unlawful to harass a person because of that person's sex. Harassment can include "sexual harassment" or unwelcome sexual advances, requests for sexual favors, and other verbal or physical harassment of a sexual nature. Harassment does not have to be of a sexual nature, however, and can include offensive remarks about a person's sex. For example, it is illegal to harass a woman by making offensive comments about women in general.

Although the law doesn't prohibit simple teasing, offhand comments, or isolated incidents that are not very serious, harassment is illegal when the offensive behavior is so frequent or severe that it creates a hostile or offensive work environment, or when it results in an adverse employment decision (such as the victim's being fired or demoted). The harasser can be the victim's supervisor, a supervisor in another area, a co-worker, or someone who is not an employee of the employer, such as a client or customer. Both victim and the harasser can be either a woman or a man, and the victim and harasser can be the same sex. The bottom line is if you are made uncomfortable by a co-worker or manager's unwelcome and repeated sexual remarks or advances, you are experiencing sexual harassment.

Sometimes harassment is subtle. Several of the women whose stories are shared here experienced some version of being told to wear a skirt (or show cleavage) for a customer meeting or trade show booth duty. This implies that your primary value is as a sex object—because sex sells—and takes away from your intelligence or skills.

In one office where I worked, one of my male coworkers was very flirtatious and made his way through the office giving back massages to many of the women. He frequently made inappropriate sexual remarks with no regard for who was listening. According to the law, Lou's behavior could be judged as creating a hostile work environment for me, even if I was not directly a recipient of the massages or a target of the inappropriate remarks. When I mentioned to management that his behavior made me uncomfortable, I was told, "That's just Lou. He's basically harmless." It shouldn't have come as a surprise when I experienced gender discrimination later, as women were not valued in that company.

While sexual harassment is a huge topic worthy of its own books, I acknowledge it here as an indicator of larger problems. We need to be aware of all ways women are treated in the workplace. You need to understand the laws that protect you, and to talk with Human Resources or your manager if your rights are being violated. Document what is said to you and how your company handles your complaints.

Becky, an IT dynamo

Becky, a director of marketing communications at an IT company, had established herself as a star—a hard-working, smart team player who got the job done. She had a solid reputation and connections within her organization long before they hired a new VP of marketing. The VP was hired to manage six directors, each with teams under them, though he had never managed people before and didn't know the business. Instead of relying on his seasoned team of directors (four women and two men), within six months he brought in new team members, his own "yes people."

"He clearly and visibly picked sides," she recounts. "All the people that bowed down and kowtowed to him were on the right side. All that questioned him, 'What are we trying to do?' got on his bad side, because they were exposing him—not that we were trying to take him down; we were trying to get work done. He wouldn't come to meetings. He started promoting supporters and writing up non-supporters." By not kowtowing to the new VP, Becky found herself on the wrong side. Her experience and knowledge were a threat to his ego.

Six months after he arrived, he came to Becky with a damaging performance review. "Now you're going to tell me, after five years, that I'm a problem. He told me all this stuff I was doing that was hearsay from his 'good side' people. 'She's holding secret meetings,' etc.—none of it true—completely damaging." Becky did the smart thing and asked the VP to send her an email on what he thought she needed to work on and how they could move forward from this.

Document everything

Any time you feel you are being treated unfairly, get as much information as you can in writing, even if it is just to write down what was said to you and when. By asking the VP to email what he saw were Becky's shortcomings, she had formal documentation of what was being said, so she could counter it with her own evidence. This also is a reminder of why you need to document your successes and accomplishments throughout your career, so if there is ever any question, you can quickly refer to your "brag folder."

Take it to Human Resources

Beyond making smart moves on her own, Becky went immediately to HR with her concerns. She brought her review, along with a list of her accomplishments over the past six months as well as the past six years at the company. She knew the VP's complaints were unfounded, and she had evidence to support her argument. She laid it all out before the HR representative. "She was very supportive, but she was not going to fight the battle. She recommended I hold a skip level meeting with the senior vice president."

Take it to the top

Becky went to meet with the senior VP. "We had a great meeting; he clearly knew my work. I make sure people know what I'm doing. I told him, 'This is what I see, what I believe is a discrepancy in how my work is being viewed. I'm willing to fix it, but we are clearly crossing some lines here from an HR perspective.' I didn't say it, but he knew what I was talking about."

Becky had grounds at this point to lodge a discrimination complaint, but the senior VP took a different approach: "You know what I think this is? It's a personality clash." At this point, Becky was fuming. "'Call it what you will,' I said. 'How do you suggest I solve it?' He had a couple of suggestions, some good, some not. I said, 'I will take these, but I want to go on record here. I find it hard to believe that after five years of success and promotions that suddenly there's a problem, and it's *me*. It seems kind of odd that this happens overnight in six months when the only factor changing is the new VP.'"

A losing battle

At this point, Becky knew she was going to have a battle on her hands, and she was unlikely to come out the winner against the new VP. She also saw that they would find ways to justify the complaints against her, even with something as lame as a "personality clash." She went back to her work, continuing to document what she was doing and what he was saying to her and about her. She also started looking for another job.

Over Christmas, she got the word there was going to be a restructure. The VP was plotting to move up his favorites—those who spent their time waiting on him, sitting in his office, telling him how great he was. There was speculation of affairs. Coworkers and colleagues stopped trusting each other.

The VP decided to restructure, planning to demote Becky and taking away parts of her job not needed any more. Becky was clear that this had not been discussed among management, and he was operating in a vacuum. She told him, "If you are serious, let's talk about what we are going to do, my title, and are you touching my pay?" She wanted to document it all.

She went back to the senior VP to tell him about the restructuring. Meanwhile at HR, she told them she was not going to stand for this. "HR was not supporting it but not stopping it. They were checking in with me, 'Are you okay?' They knew I had a case and wanted to shut me up."

HR's hands are sometimes tied

Unfortunately, Human Resources is often caught in a bind when there is an issue within the company. They are motivated to work things out and to calm the employees who are having issues so that they will not bring a discrimination lawsuit. They are also supposed to work with management to minimize complaints and correct issues as they occur—but this is often difficult to do with a headstrong or powerful executive.

Before the Christmas break, Becky told the VP, "Why don't you take the break, get it all worked out with HR, put it in writing—what the package you're offering me is going to look like and what we will tell staff. After the holidays, we will come back and straighten it out." He was thrilled. In his mind, he thought the issues were settled and Becky was no longer a problem.

Moving on

But Becky knew she was on a final interview to leave the company. "He was going to take me down regardless. He got it all documented over the holiday, called me into his office to tell me all about it. I brought my letter in. I just want you to know I resign; my last date will be x. I really hope this works out for you, and this new structure works in your favor, because I will no longer be here. Good luck."

The VP turned white. Suddenly everyone was asking what had happened, and why someone as valuable as Becky was resigning. The CEO came to see her. "I'd love to get some time with you before you go, make sure things are good, you are on your way" (read: make sure no lawsuit was coming). At this point, the volcano was bubbling, and he knew there were bigger problems. "I'm really challenged by the fact you are leaving when we are paying out bonuses in three weeks. Why would you do that?"

"Some things are bigger than money. That bonus is not worth my jeopardizing my new opportunity." He looked at me like I was crazy. "You guys are toxic. I can't do this anymore." But we had a frank discussion. I told him, "You have management problems, leadership issues, things that go on. I gave data points that could be supported by facts by HR, didn't name names or do 'he said, she said,' but just said, "This isn't the environment for me. I need to be somewhere that they value work ethic and output, and that is not the case here."

Six months after Becky left for her new opportunity, she found out her former VP had been fired. That's how long they took to correct the problem. "That was the one time I was taken to the mat, because I was trying to do a job and produce results. There are times to be aggressive and not, but this was so blatantly discriminatory—whether it's personality or whatever, it doesn't matter—for anybody. He was a piece of work."

What else could be done?

Becky used her knowledge of her rights to fight back, until it became clear she was in a no-win situation. She did everything right—asking the new VP what she needed to do to improve, documenting everything, going to HR with her concerns, going to her senior VP, and working on things that were within her control. Once she realized she was not getting full support from HR or senior management and that they were going to tolerate this behavior from their VP, she made the choice to move on. Sometimes changing the game is better than to continuing to fight.

Could she have chosen to fight this in the courts as a discrimination case? This would have come with big challenges. Others who were being promoted were women, so it wasn't clear that gender was an issue. Her experience, connections, and the respect others had for her in her workplace worked against her in this case, as she became a threat to the new guy. In some ways, it *was* a personality clash—in that her VP wanted people working for him that kowtowed to his needs, and Becky was unwilling to compromise her work to do that.

Laws as a tool

Knowing your rights doesn't mean you threaten to sue every time someone starts to violate them. This knowledge just gives you another tool in the toolbox for fighting back. Employers don't want to violate the law, or at least, they don't want to get caught violating it. Sometimes just by letting them know *you* know it's a violation, you can get them to change. The fear of a lawsuit or even an uncomfortable conversation with management or HR can be a strong motivator to toe the line.

If you find yourself in a discriminatory situation, your first stop should be HR. They are supposed to be your advocate, and they are tasked with advising the management team on best practices for avoiding discrimination, sexual harassment, etc. If you get no satisfaction from HR or top management, you can choose to pursue your case with an attorney, or by filing a discrimination charge with the EEOC. If you have questions, Equal Rights Advocates (ERA) has a multilingual Advice and Counseling Line that you can call to receive free practical advice and information about your legal rights. See www.equalrights.org. There are other advocacy groups for specific industries or organizations as well. Alternatively, you can choose to move out of the toxic environment to one better suited for your advancement. There is not one right answer that fits everyone.

Feeling trapped

What if you can't afford to change jobs? Sometimes a change would mean a significant financial impact—whether giving up on a bonus, seniority, vacation time, or 401K vesting. Also, when the economy is suffering, and jobs are harder to find, you may not want to put yourself out there. Walking away is not always the best option.

This is when it is most important to address—carefully—the issues that are making you want to leave.

1. Start with Human Resources, if the role exists in your company. This can be a confidential conversation where you air your grievances and they provide advice. Often they can strategize with you on ways to approach your manager or coworker to discuss the issues. Someone who knows the people involved may more easily be able to provide you with helpful advice.

2. If you don't have an HR department, or you are not comfortable approaching them, try to find a mentor or other person who can help you navigate the specific issues with the goal of improving the situation rather than leaving it.

3. With your documentation to back you up, approach your manager or coworker with your concerns. Keep it positive, stating that you are concerned but are looking for ways to improve the relationship. Bringing positive solutions is always more helpful than just complaining. For example, you could say, "I was disappointed that Harry got the promotion rather than me, when I feel I am more qualified. What can I do to improve my qualifications to allow for future growth? Do you have any specific concerns I need to address?" As much as you may want to rant and rave, you will likely achieve more by giving the other person an opportunity to respond with positive suggestions. At the same time, you are

letting them know that you noticed the promotion was possibly unfair and given notice that you want equal opportunities in the future.

Keep the faith

Witnessing or being a victim of sex discrimination or sexual harassment can be very demoralizing. You may be frustrated that we continue to fight this fight more than 50 years after laws were passed to protect women and others against discrimination. But we have made progress. Women play an increasingly important role in the workplace. We are moving up, changing the dynamic in formerly male-dominated professions, and slowly closing the pay gap. The more we stand up for our rights and serve notice either formally or informally to those who are violating them, the more progress we will make.

In your individual situation, don't lose sight of your own dignity. You are smart, skilled, and motivated to succeed. Know your rights and start with the fact that you are entitled to be treated with respect and rewarded based on your achievements and capabilities just as much as the next person. Even if you have to go up against your employer, be strong in the face of attacks on your personal power.

CHAPTER 7

THE SAVVY WORKING MOTHER

IF A SMART WORKING WOMAN becomes a threat to the status quo by wanting to move up within an organization, she finds a new block in her way if she chooses to continue this drive after having children.

The special challenge of the working mother

According to the U.S. Department of Labor, almost 47% of U.S. workers are women.[3] Seventy percent of women with children under 18 are in the labor force, with over 75% of them working full time. Yes, this is becoming more acceptable. But there are still many people who judge working mothers as bad mothers and/or bad workers.

Once a woman has children, if she decides to return to work, she finds herself challenging another deeply held assumption by many men and women: *mothers should stay home with their children.* And if

---

3   U.S. Department of Labor Blog. "12 Stats About Working Women." Blog.dol.gov. https://blog.dol.gov/2017/03/01/12-stats-about-working-women (accessed October 8. 2019).

a woman chooses to continue to work, some people will assume it is because she *has to*, not because she *wants to*. Her desire to work hard and move up within the organization, all while raising a family, makes her a target from all sides. Both men and women, at work and at home and in the community, may see her as a threat to the status quo and will place obstacles in her path.

At work, they may assume that she will scale back on her hours, not work as hard, or is likely to quit work to stay home with her children. Suddenly career options become limited, advancement opportunities are scarce, and she finds herself defending her choices to her coworkers and managers. Even if her own work ethic and abilities have not changed, she may find her managers downshifting her career, perhaps making the choice for her that she needs to spend more time at home.

At home, a husband who was formerly supportive of his wife's career ambitions might have different views once they have children. He may decide she should scale back on her career to raise the children or just be less involved than he could be, leaving her to bear the complete burden of childcare on top of everything else.

In her community, a career-oriented mother might find herself excluded from the group of mothers who stay home with their children. Also, her children may be excluded from friendships in the neighborhood, while they are off in day care all day.

If that's not challenge enough. . .

If a woman becomes a threat to the status quo by wanting to move up within an organization, she reaches a new level if she chooses to continue this drive *after* having children.

It's one thing to be a working mother; lots of people do it, after all. Plenty of women go back to work after an acceptable maternity leave, and everyone knows she would much rather be at home with the baby, but gosh, we all have to make a living. But as soon as this working mother puts in extra hours on a project, seeks a promotion, or generally strives to move forward with her career, the acceptance goes way down. Even if she has a supportive husband or great child-care, her community may judge her unfairly as a "bad mother."

Managers or coworkers may be put off by a woman's ambitions "at the expense of her children." Or they may resent having to "take up the slack" on days when a working mother needs to take time off with a sick child.

Guilt

One of the most pervasive and destructive forces in this war on the ambitious working mother is guilt. Anyone who is a parent knows the challenges and doubts that creep in on whether they are being a "good mother" or "good father." Society's expectations, advertising, television, and movies all reinforce the message. Just one friend's posting on Facebook about an educational outing with her kids or Pinterest suggestions for how to make the perfect casserole or home-made Halloween costume when all you can manage is McDonald's and a store-bought mask—it doesn't take much to turn on the guilt. Depending on how you your own mother raised you, she might criticize your decision to leave your children in someone else's care while you work. Your neighbors, friends, church community, and others may lay their judgments on you, adding to the guilty feelings.

Compound that guilt with what you might feel at work when you need to leave a project unfinished for a day because it's time to pick up the children from day care. Because one thing I know about smart, ambitious women: we don't like to do a poor job—at anything.

But it can be done

I did it, as did Judy, Connie, and Valerie—all ambitious working mothers. We suffered the judgments of our colleagues, managers, neighbors, and even family and friends. We found resources to help us, though, and fought off the guilt that comes from making choices every day to leave home or to leave work before we should. Because it was important to us to both be good parents and to advance our careers. Valerie and I were single parents for a good portion of our children's lives. Judy and Connie had supportive husbands. Regardless of your situation, you can make it work.

Managing the workload

At its simplest level, the first challenge of an ambitious working mother is managing the workload. In some ways, raising a family is another set of tasks on a woman's to-do list: pick up diapers, feed the baby, go to work, cook dinner, read a bedtime story. *Check.* Depending on how much help she has—how much she can delegate to the children's father, a nanny, family members, or others—the additional needs could be overwhelming on top of a full-time, possibly high-stress job. Even before the baby is born, she may be interviewing and visiting daycare centers or nannies, arranging coverage at work for while she is out on maternity leave, and outfitting her nursery for the new arrival.

Trying to do it all

I knew that it wouldn't be easy, working and wanting to advance my career after having children, but I had never been afraid of hard work. I was going to have it all, and nobody could stop me. When I became pregnant with my son, I was working full-time as an engineer and going to school at night for my master's degree in electrical engineering. I was making as much or more money than my husband *and* going home at night to cook dinner and clean the house. He mowed the lawn in the summer and took out the trash when it was overflowing, then parked in front of the television. I propped up my rapidly swelling feet in the evening with my communications theory book in front of me, trying to remember how to do integration by parts while fighting sleepiness in the first trimester and plain exhaustion in the third trimester. For work, I squeezed into my maternity panty hose and ever-tightening pumps and tried to find maternity dresses that didn't have little bows on them declaring my girliness.

Why? Because I still had a serious job and serious intentions to do it well and be respected for it. As lead systems engineer on a large hardware and software project, I needed to know how everything worked and how each person's technical details fit into the whole. I was in my element and loved every part of my job. My mind was challenged every day, and I was energized by my work.

Trying to do most of it

As my son's due date approached, though, something had to give. As exhausted as I was at the end of my pregnancy, I knew that the situation wouldn't get much better after the baby arrived. I worried about being able to keep up with everything, and I told my husband he was going to have to help out more after the baby was born (wishful thinking, unfortunately). To alleviate some of the pressure, I decided to take a semester off from my master's degree studies.

I spent hours researching the best caregiver options for my baby before he was born and decided on home-based care in a provider's home. I interviewed and visited multiple people, shuddering at the condition of some homes and the attitudes of the women watching the children. Eventually, I settled on a lovely woman with a couple small children of her own who was watching a couple more. I could tell by the way she interacted with the children and how they responded to her that she would love my baby and care for him in a warm and safe environment.

Can she do it . . . and with two children?

I'd seen myself as a capable woman, mainly because I knew myself to be a hard worker. The question was, could I manage the workload of both family and career, still getting where I wanted to go? And how quickly could I recover from a C-section and get back to my career so as not to miss a beat and face the supposition that I was now "behind" or that I'd "lost touch."

At work, I jumped back into my systems engineering responsibilities and moved up to program manager of this multimillion-dollar project. After my semester off and a summer off, I continued my education at night, taking one engineering class per semester toward my master's degree. After another baby 3½ years later, I had a son and a daughter I could go home to at night for hugs and laughter, as well as diapers and crying. I left work promptly at 5:00 to get home to my children and studied after they went to sleep at night. My husband was content to let me continue to cook and clean and now care for the children, occasionally pitching in when things hit crisis stage. I finished my master's degree, proudly walking in the ceremony with my children in the audience, hoping nobody would need a diaper change before I received my diploma.

So far, so good. I was managing it all. I'd worked hard and was willing to keep working hard to achieve my goals. Everything was moving along as planned, or so I thought.

Yes, she can!

At work, I was on fire. The program I was managing was hugely successful, and we received a letter of commendation from the Navy. I was named as part of the team, but three of the men who worked under me received special praise. That's just the way it was. There was no acknowledgement of my dedication when I had brought my infant daughter into work on my maternity leave, nursing her in the conference room between tests, because the acceptance testing on our hardware was scheduled.

When my boss and champion retired, he suggested me for his position, as I had proven myself more than capable of leading a team. At the age of 29, I was promoted to manager of the Engineering Department, supervising 20 engineers, most of whom were men and many of them older than I. I bought a Franklin Planner and carefully scheduled my days and tasks so I could meet my obligations at work and still get home to my children on time. This was not easy, but I was never afraid of discipline, and I was happy to be doing everything I wanted: challenging engineering work, coaching and mentoring engineers on my team, representing my project and my company in meetings, traveling occasionally for meetings and testing, and raising my children. It wasn't easy, but I was doing it.

Judgment in the workplace

What catches many women off guard when they return to work after having children is the judgment they feel from their co-workers or managers who might believe they should be staying home with their children.

Even if co-workers are supportive in theory of a mother's right to a career, they are often put off by the realities of schedule conflicts and sick children that sometimes cause disruptions. When I asked Anne, a non-mother, what she thought about working mothers, she responded, "Anyone who did have children had to do the same job that I did. You have to travel. You've got to do whatever is needed. I started finding that in the workplace, some women are starting to ask for special treatment. 'I'm a mother. I do all this. I don't want to have to travel.'" Yet when I asked the same question of Sheila, another non-mother, she said, "Most women I work with really do work hard, and this is not an issue. Your family comes first; it has to. I understand that. I never felt like I had to carry the load for them because of it." The career-oriented working mother needs to be aware of how her choices and work ethic are interpreted by others, carefully walking that fine line between the needs of her family and the demands of the job.

Others "looking out for you" . . . while derailing your career

A 2013 Pew Research Center survey[4] found that, among parents with at least some work experience, mothers with children under age 18 were about three times as likely as fathers to say that being a working parent made it harder for them to advance in their job or career (51% vs. 16%). Judy, a project manager in a large telecommunications company, also decided to continue to advance her career while having children. She had been with the company since its infancy, working hard and proving herself as a smart and ambitious contributor. When Judy was about six weeks away from her due date on her second child, she lumbered into her manager's office for a

---

4   Parker, Kim, Rich Morin, and D'Vera Cohn. "On Pay Gap, Millennial Women Near Parity—For Now." PewSocialTrends.org. https://www.pewsocialtrends. org/2013/12/11/on-pay-gap-millennial-women-near-parity-for-now/ (accessed October 16, 2019).

status meeting. Carol looked up with a smile as she entered. "How are you feeling?"

Judy sat down with a sigh, leaning back into the chair to make room for her growing belly. "Tired but fine." She looked down at her swollen ankles and twisted them around a bit to increase circulation. She leaned forward. "I wanted to update you on my project. I just got the test results back, and everything is looking good for launch."

Carol smiled. "That's great news, Judy. I knew I could count on you once again. You always get the job done." She paused while Judy thanked her for the compliment. "That's why it's so disappointing I can't give you the new team leader position. You would have gotten the role, but with your going on maternity leave soon, we didn't think the timing was right for you."

Judy was caught in the all-too-common trap of others' deciding what is best for her and her family. Rather than asking Judy whether she wanted the position, her manager simply assumed she would not want to take on the extra work while raising her children—or she was implying that the company could not trust her to do both.

Judy's jaw dropped open slightly, and she put her hand on her stomach, trying to determine if the knot formed there was from disappointment or the baby kicking. She had wanted the team leader role and felt she had earned it. Though her planned 3-month maternity leave would present challenges, it could have been worked around. She hadn't anticipated this being a factor in their decision not to promote her. After sitting stunned for a few minutes while Carol talked about the upcoming project, Judy excused herself and returned to her office.

Wow, I can't believe they took my maternity leave into account when deciding on this promotion, she thought. *But she's probably right: You can't put me into a new position, then have me go out for three months and come back, because you're trying to start something new. There is plenty of work to do, and I'm sure when I return from leave, I will have more opportunities to advance.* Judy shook off her disappointment and told her husband about it when she got home.

The next day, when a coworker asked about why Judy didn't get the team leader position, Judy just shrugged and said, "Oh, she passed me over because I'm going on maternity leave." That's when the trouble started. Either someone overheard the comment, or the coworker was upset about it and brought the issue up with Human Resources, who were forced to address it under the company's Standards of Conduct policy. Judy was called in to discuss it with Carol's boss. According to Judy:

> He called me in, was aware of the situation, and asked what I wanted to do about it. I didn't want to do anything about it. I didn't report it in the first place. Carol got a hand slapping, and she and I talked about it. I was apologetic to her, because I didn't want it to take that channel and go to Standards of Business Conduct. I apologized for any negative repercussions that she might have suffered as a result. She was fine with it. But it was a really strange situation. I wish she hadn't said that to me in the first place, because I don't think it would have been an issue.

Set the expectation

Could Judy have gotten ahead of this problem, before others decided what was best for her? If she were more knowledgeable about what to expect in the workplace, she might have declared her intentions in advance about working after her maternity leave. Even as she announced her pregnancy, she could have said, "I don't expect this to impact my work life beyond my maternity leave." If she knew the promotion was a possibility, she could have put her name in for consideration rather than *hope* they would promote her. Hope is not a strategy.

Once she found herself passed over for the promotion, she could have gone to HR herself to discuss it. She might have talked with HR about what she did and did not want to happen as a result of this—including whether she wanted her manager's "hand slapped."

The best way to show that you are in charge of your own career, no matter the circumstances, is to take charge. If you are considering family leave, let your manager know your intentions for during and after your pregnancy or leave. Be clear about what time you will need off, whether you want to come back to work part time for a while and then transition to full time, or if you plan to come back full time right away. If you have set an expectation, managers will find it harder to justify decisions that are based on a different assumption. However, be aware that, depending on the biases of your manager, they may not believe you when you say you will be back in full force. Remain watchful of how you are being treated before and after your leave to make sure their internal biases are not contradicting your actual behavior.

Don't tell me how to balance my work and family

Valerie, the VP of IT in an insurance company, finds it frustrating when others want to decide for her what she can and can't do. "I'm in a unique situation. I balance home, kids, and work. But I often get, 'Are you going to be able to come to this out-of-town meeting, or do you have something with the family?' Balancing my family is my job; you don't worry about that. You tell me what the business job is. I will figure out my personal schedule."

Valerie has heard from the president of her company, "Family is more important than business, so if you have something that you need to do with your family, then we'll skip this." She doesn't like to hear that. "Don't make accommodations for me because I'm a mother—because down the road, something's going to happen, and that's going to hurt me. I often want to say, 'You've got three kids at home. Do you make these accommodations?'"

Even when she was a single mom, she figured it all out. "You just figure it out. If I know a band concert is coming up next Thursday, I'll get my work done Monday/Tuesday/Wednesday. Or if I have an out-of-town trip, I figure it out—arrange a carpool or whatever. And it goes both ways. Sometimes I'm not 100% mom, or 100% work. Give and take. But that's my job to figure that out; it's not their job to figure it out."

Savvy women set the expectation that they can manage their own work-life balance. When Valerie hears her executive management ask whether her family commitments will get in the way of work, she needs to be clear: "Don't make accommodations for me because I'm a mother." It sounds *nice* of the president to say family is more important than work, right? The reality is, if she takes advantage of that too often, she will be seen as less committed to her job.

If you talk incessantly about your children at work, that is how you are identified in the workplace. The more calls you take from your children during the day, the less committed you appear. This is not to say you have to pretend to be something you are not. But if, as a mother, you are choosing to pursue a career, you need to be sure that your coworkers and managers see you as a career woman first.

If you are excelling on the job and making sure others are aware of what you are doing, they are less likely to judge you as less dedicated after having children. Then, when you inevitably need to take time off with a sick child, that will be less likely to impact you.

The downshift decision

Judy might have been more upset, but when she started having kids, she made a conscious decision to downshift her career for a while. She passed up other opportunities. She did work hard and still had a lot of passion for the work that she was doing, but she wasn't interested in moving up the career ladder at that point, and she limited her hours to no more than 45 per week.

"In hindsight, I don't know if I would have made the same decision again, because downshifting and taking that approach may have hurt my career—especially since it was during my thirties, which is when a lot of men and women are at the height of their career, when they start to pull forward in the organizations they work for. It made me look like I lacked ambition, at least in the company. For me personally, I felt like it was the right choice, because my family was more important to me at that time than my career was."

This is a decision many women struggle with, and there is no one answer that is right for everyone. Unfortunately, the reality is that if you step back from work even a little due to family obligations, you can be seen as not being dedicated to the job. This affects women much more than it does men.

Valerie has seen it in her business: "We talk about job sharing and working from home—those things—but it's not as prevalent. Those women that do that are obviously looked over. The thinking is, *You've made the choice to work from home to look after the kids; you're not devoted to your job.* You hurt yourself."

It gets crazier: Even if you don't change your hours, and you work extra hard while you are there, you may be lumped in with other women who have made the decision to cut back. That happened to me, much to my surprise and detriment.

Digging back in

With the support of her husband, Judy stayed in the workforce, taking three-month maternity leaves for each of her three children. Then once her children were a little older, and she was ready to shift into high gear, she did. She was promoted within a year and a half after she made the decision, "I'm going after it again." She worked long hours to prove herself and show that she was dedicated—working from 8 to 8 several nights a week for six months after her promotion, plus time on the weekends.

"I really burned myself out. It was hard on me, hard on the family. Fortunately, Paul is very supportive; he's home taking care of the kids. That helped a lot. Did it pay off? I don't know. Will I get a promotion out of it? I don't know. Other than my boss' knowing that I was working really hard."

Judy made the decision to put in the extra hours to prove she was a dedicated and hard-working employee. At the time, she felt that was necessary. If she had chosen not to, would it have made a difference? Possibly. But that was her choice to make, with her husband's support.

Whose decision is it?

The work required for a smart, ambitious woman to move up in her career while raising a family is enormous and not for everyone. Many women make the decision to downshift a little during their children's early years, then ramp back up when the kids are in school. It is one thing for a woman to make that choice, and quite another for her coworkers and managers to assume she doesn't want or deserve a promotion simply because she has children at home.

While I never consciously decided to sideline my career ambitions, I did try to honor the 40-hour work week and respect the needs of my family. When deadlines or issues demanded it, I worked late or on weekends but generally tried to fit everything into the business day. And during my working hours, I brought my dedication, intelligence, leadership, and ambition to the job, fully expecting that this was the way to move forward with my career. I didn't realize how my motherhood would affect my upward mobility, but I would soon find out.

Guilt—from all sides and inside

Returning to work after my son was born was a challenge, and I won't say that there was not some guilt there, leaving my baby at the sitter's each morning. I will say without apology, though, that I never considered not going back to work. I had worked too hard for my education, and I loved my job and the feeling I got when using my mind to face technical challenges. We also needed the money, but it wasn't only that. I needed work and the refreshing of my spirit it brought me to be a better mother when I got home to my son. I made sure he was in a loving and safe environment and nursed him morning and night, relaxing into the moments with him as he gazed up into my eyes.

At the same time, I was beginning to see the landscape ahead of me, and it wasn't pretty. I began to see that smart working women who were also mothers got nailed from all sides. The guilt would come like a ball in the back of my throat when 5:00 arrived and I still had A1 priority tasks unfinished on my Franklin planner due to interruptions or other priorities that snuck in during the day. But then I would picture my daughter smiling up at me, her pacifier dropping from her mouth, or my son ready to run into my arms and animatedly tell me the story of his day. I would swallow the guilt, move the task to the next day, close the planner, and head home. There would always be more work than time to complete it, but my children would not always be small.

Or the guilt would come when one of my friends or neighbors, perhaps a stay-at-home mom, would ask me, "How can you leave your children to go to work? I could never do that." The knot would form in my stomach as I thought of all the ways I was a bad mother, and I would find myself justifying, defending, and trying to explain. I loved my children, of course. I wanted the very best for them, but I came to realize that for me to be the very best mom, I needed to be happy and fulfilled myself. I would think about not going to work— not coaching engineers, solving technical problems, or presenting our results to the customer—and the same ball would form in the back of my throat and threaten to choke me.

This is one of the greatest challenges working mothers face, and it is both an external and internal challenge. The decision to stay in the workforce after having children is attacked from all sides—other women's judging you as a bad mother, men's thinking you should be staying home, other employees' looking at the clock when you leave at the end of the day.

How children benefit from working mothers

I wish I had known this years ago when I was struggling with the guilt of being a working mother. I read the headline last week, and

I had to sit down and breathe. "Working moms have more successful daughters and more caring sons, Harvard Business School study says."[5]

According to the study, done in June 2015, "Daughters of working mothers are more likely to be employed, hold supervisory positions, and earn more money than the daughters of women who don't work outside the home. The researchers also found a statistically significant effect on the sons of working women, who are likely to spend more time caring for family members and doing household chores than are the sons of stay-at-home mothers."

Could it be that, contrary to popular belief, my children were actually better off from having me work? I had always felt that way, even with the guilt, as I knew I was a better mother by having the outlet of working. I was also modeling for my daughter how to have a career and expecting my son to pitch in around the house rather than expect me to do everything. Maybe Harvard is onto something.

Kathleen McGinn, a professor at Harvard Business School and the lead author of the study, was surprised to find that having a working mother even positively affected daughters' chances of being a supervisor at work. The study found that 33% of daughters of working mothers held supervisory roles compared to only 25% of daughters of stay-at-home moms. "What I take away is that employed mothers create an environment in which their children's attitudes on what is appropriate for girls to do and what is appropriate for boys to do is affected," McGinn says.

Well, how about that? I was not the worst mother ever.

---

5   Fisher, Gabriel. "Working moms have more successful daughters and more caring sons, Harvard Business School study says." Quartz.com. https://qz.com/434056/working-moms-have-more-successful-daughters-and-more-caring-sons-harvard-business-school-study-says/ (accessed October 16, 2019).

Making this very personal choice

Sticking with a decision to stay in the work force takes enormous reserves of courage, courage that is needed on a daily or even hourly basis. I believe that this very personal choice should be regarded as such and that we should allow women to make their own choices without judgment. Nobody questions that a man will continue to work after his wife gives birth. Nobody considers that he is being a bad father by earning a living. Instead, a man is congratulated when he leaves work to attend a child's baseball game, because he is being a good dad. When a woman takes a day off because her child is sick or sends the child to day care with a stuffy nose, she is either being a bad employee or a bad mother—or perhaps both.

I have many smart women friends who made the other choice—to give up or sideline their careers to raise their families. I admire them for their commitment and am thankful to them, for they are the volunteers in our schools and communities. If they judge me as a bad mother, they mostly keep it to themselves, and I am thankful for that.

What I will say to young women facing this choice is this: Listen to your own heart and tune out the chatter from society. Know what you need and where that will take you, and own it. The more confidence you have in your decision, the happier you will be, and the quieter the naysayers will be.

Be prepared

If you choose to stay in the workforce, prepare for changes and battles you may not have anticipated. Do not be surprised if your colleagues and managers look at you differently and judge you from their own beliefs and biases. Even if you are a smart, ambitious woman with an advanced degree who works hard before and after children, some people may be expecting you to drop out to raise your children on any given day. Even if you work the same hours you did before children, you may find others questioning your work ethic. If you need to take a day off occasionally to care for a sick child, you may return to find colleagues or your manager looking down their nose at you or complaining that they had to take up your slack. If you need to travel for your job, some people may judge you for going on the trip and leaving your children at home with their father or other caregiver, and others may judge you for choosing not to and neglecting work. Performance reviews may be more critical and pay raises scarcer.

But if it is important to you, there are ways to combat all of this. You may need to work even harder and be more vocal about what you are accomplishing to overcome the biases you will encounter, but that doesn't mean you cannot still be a successful woman both at work and at home.

CHAPTER 8

THREAT TO EGO AND FIGHTING BACK

Women as a threat to ego

We've seen how women can become a threat to the *status quo*—by moving into roles formerly held by men, by questioning unfair salary practices, or in a variety of other ways. We have also found that by being smarter, better positioned, more assertive, savvier, or more respected, we can become a threat to the ego of a colleague or manager. This, as some of us have experienced, can result in the same tactics' being used against us.

Sometimes the first and best response to these tactics is to fight back. This can be done in bold or subtle ways to suit your personality, but we all must adopt savvy techniques to combat the forces against us if we are to move forward in our careers.

Even if you don't mean to be a threat, you are

Anyone, male or female, can become a threat to the ego of a colleague or manager, male or female. Nobody particularly likes it when someone appears to be better than him or her in some way.

I would posit, however, that a smart woman is often perceived as more of a threat to a man's or woman's ego than a smart man would be, simply because she is a woman. Here's how that plays out in my own experience:

Back at my company, my education, intelligence, and hard work were paying off, but they also made me a threat. My director, Dick, had a non-technical bachelor's degree and was more of a people manager than a technical contributor. He was no dummy by any means, but he was not an engineer. With my master's degree in electrical engineering, strong technical skills, program management experience, and no hesitation in putting forth my opinions, it's possible I was a threat to Dick's ego, in addition to threatening the status quo. Based on some of the tactics he used against me—more on that later—I highly suspect that was the case.

Again, I was far from alone in this. Rosa, a highly respected and successful lawyer who has written law reference books in her area of expertise for years, frequently poses a threat to the egos of some of her colleagues and partners. Petite and pretty, Rosa makes up for her small size with a big personality, brains, and a feisty manner. She is often asked for advice by other attorneys in her firm and has no problem pointing out to them when their opinions are wrong in her area of expertise. While most are happy to take her advice, others do not take it well.

After Connie (a former dental hygienist) helped build a new company in a collaborative, entrepreneurial environment, she worked her way up to being vice president. All was well until they needed to hire a safety expert, Jack. Jack came in and instantly resented her experience, knowledge, and position as vice president. He did not like taking orders from a woman. Connie didn't want to believe it, but by being smarter and better positioned in the company she had helped grow, she had become a threat to the ego of Jack, the new guy.

When Karen was hired as the director of human resources at the automotive group, she came in above Sally, who was previously doing the job as a manager of HR. Sally thought they were replacing her. Karen recalls,

> She thought I was a threat to her. That wasn't the case. The company was growing rapidly, and they decided they needed more personnel. It took me a long time to reassure her I wasn't going to take her job. I would call her and say "Can you come to my office?" She would come in quivering with fear. I had to start saying, "Can you come in, and we can discuss such and such?" so she wouldn't feel like I was going to fire her. It's sad. It took a long time to convince her, "No, we're not going to fire you. You have to act right, but we're not going to fire you."

> Karen didn't mean to be a threat to Sally, but Sally saw her that way.

All you have to do is want to move up . . . and possibly past others

Being a smart woman is one thing, but if you really want to get someone's goat, be ambitious. Many people are comfortable enough with men and women who are smarter or more capable than they, as long as we stay in our place. But when we start to seek promotions, put ourselves out there for choice assignments, higher visibility, and movement up the career ladder, we can become more of a threat to the egos of our colleagues and managers.

When women take on previously male-dominated roles in their careers, teasing out the difference between being a threat to the status quo and a threat to someone's ego can be difficult. Knowing which it is which may not be important, as the tactics used against women are generally the same.

If you're more connected/respected than someone else, you're a double threat

As clever women, we are often well connected and respected by our colleagues and managers after demonstrating our talents and work ethic. This is important for advancing our careers. Unfortunately, this very connectedness can pose a threat to the egos of others. When Shirley's company reorganized, and they brought in a female director from another division, the new director resented Shirley's connections and experience within the division. Shirley was a threat to the new woman's ego, and she would soon find herself a target of her new director's tactics.

Don't kowtow to others who want you to do their work for them

Successful women are not "yes women." We don't always agree with what others are saying, and we don't mind telling them. We don't always agree to do work that is outside our scope just to help someone else look good. This can be a serious threat to the ego of a manager who thinks he or she knows it all and wants to be surrounded by blind followers.

As discussed in the last chapter, Becky, a director of marketing communications at an IT company, had established a strong reputation and connections within her organization long before they hired a new vice president of marketing. Becky continued to do her good work and challenged some of his decisions based on her knowledge and history with the company. When the VP started promoting the people who always said "yes" and never challenged him, Becky found herself on his wrong side. Her experience and knowledge were a threat to his ego, and he was going to find a way to put her in her place.

Fighting back

There are many ways—both subtle and not-so-subtle—to fight back against people who try to keep you from moving ahead. In the previous chapter, Becky used her knowledge of her rights to take her fight to Human Resources and bring in upper management to see if she could prevail against her new VP. Her ultimate decision to move on was made after she put up a good fight and realized she was no longer interested in doing battle at that company.

Start by being excellent

The very things that make you a threat to the ego of a colleague or manager—your know-how, intelligence, experience, and capability—must be the basis of your ability to fight back against tactics that are used against you. Use your strengths. If you are excellent at your job, and you know it and others know it, you will have much more success deflecting blows against you. It is much harder for a colleague to bad-mouth you if others already know the strength of your work. If you come from a position of weakness, either because you lack confidence in your abilities or you need to build skills in a certain area, you will have a harder time.

Becky knew she had a strong reputation at her company before the new VP came on board, and she was confident in her abilities. This gave her the confidence and strength to fight back against his inequitable treatment.

Make small corrections

Sometimes a short conversation is enough to correct a situation. Not everything requires a full-on battle. When I first started a job a while ago, I worked with an inside salesman who supported me while I was out in the field. He was based on the West Coast, and I was on the East Coast, but we communicated regularly by phone, email, and messages. For the most part, we got along great. First, I noticed he referred to the other sales operations staff as "the girls," which I thought was a little disrespectful. I let it slide, thinking perhaps this was a generational thing and the young women there might not mind it. When he started messaging me with "Hey Girly" and "Okay Girly," however, I knew I had to stop it.

"'Girly' is not going to work for me," I messaged him.

"It's a term of endearment," he responded.

"No, sorry. I don't like it."

"What can I call you then?"

"How about my name? Or if that's too long, my initials."

"Okay, fine, ME."

No blood was shed, and we continued to work well together without his calling me "Girly."

Stand your ground

I recently ran into another situation where a big fight wasn't warranted, but smaller adjustments needed to be made. I moved to a new company where I was responsible for sales in a certain region that had previously been covered by someone else. That person was still in the company in a different role. My tremendous success in building the territory up to record performance gave me a good reputation in the company—and possibly threatened the ego of the former salesman. We were still working together, and I noticed he kept sending snarky comments my way saying that all I cared about was charging customers for our software (which, by the way, is what my job was). I mostly just let it go, knowing he was jealous of my success and that others in the company were appreciative of my work. But then he sent an insulting email, copying others, stating that since I was "sensitive" about free software, he would spell out the "big picture" for me, since clearly I didn't understand strategic investments. There were just enough insults in the email and just enough people copied on it that I couldn't just let it slide. I responded professionally but strongly enough to let him know that I didn't appreciate his tone and that I wasn't going to let him talk to me that way. We then had a candid one-on-one phone conversation where I told him specifically what my issues were. He apologized and vowed to do better.

Having the hard conversations, where you need to call someone out on their behavior, is sometimes difficult. But the longer you let the offensive behavior go on, the harder it is to change and the more damage may be done to your reputation. When I was younger, I found it much more difficult to stand up for myself in these situations. I would just cringe and try to make the best of it. Addressing it became easier as I developed confidence in my abilities, knowledge of my rights, and experience in knowing the damage that can be done by not confronting early.

Don't tolerate unacceptable behavior

Early in Becky's career, she worked for a CEO who was a bully. She wasn't going to stand for it.

> He screamed at me one time—got in my face, literally. I looked at him and said, "Michael, when you are ready to speak to me like an adult and not scream at me, we can continue this conversation." And I walked out of his office, and I closed the door—at age 24. You are not going to talk to me like that. I don't care that you are the CEO. It's not okay. I put the gauntlet down, and he didn't do it to me anymore. He continued to treat others like that, because they allowed it. I took control of the situation.

Know your own limits

Could you do that—tell the CEO not to scream at you? I'm not sure I could have at age 24, and I'd have a little trouble doing it even today, though I've not had the misfortune of being screamed at by a co-worker, thankfully. I'd like to think that if it happened, I could at least walk away until things calmed down. Then I could approach him later and try to address the issue in a civilized tone.

Some people are born fighters, and some are more apt to go along to get along. Each of us is different, and we will not all approach the same situation the same way. Knowing yourself and what you are willing to put up with can help you prepare for whatever may come your way. Also know that your attitudes may change over the course of your career, so that what you are willing to tolerate in your youth may not be the same as what you will put up with later in your career. This goes both ways: you may be more tolerant of small things and know when to pick your battles as you gain experience, or you may be more apt to fight back against injustices that had hurt you earlier in your career.

Rosa—a born fighter

Rosa came to the United States as a young girl fleeing her home country and, in the absence of her parents, was raised mostly by an aging grandmother. From an early age, she learned to take care of herself and to fight for what was hers. She went to college and law school and worked for the government for a few years before leaving to practice law in a private firm.

She was a hard worker and good lawyer, and she worked hard to build up her own client base so that she had a solid foundation if she ran into any opposition. "I was doing exactly what you're supposed to do. I was bringing in business; I was publishing; I was speaking. People were looking for me." She was a successful attorney, just a few years out of government with a solid book of business. You can bet she became a threat to the egos of some of her colleagues, but she took no shit from anyone.

Small-minded man with big ego meets smart, confident woman

Stanley, a partner in her firm, had marketed himself as a litigator, even though Rosa knew he had never been in a courtroom. Only those close in to the circle knew he had never litigated. But he always had other people do things for him. According to Rosa, "He was Mr. Ego. People thought he walked on water—at least people that were one step removed. Those close to the community knew he was an asshole but never called him on it. He hated me because I never 'sucked his dick'—so to speak."

Rosa had no problem challenging him when he was wrong, which infuriated Stanley.

> I would say, "No, honestly, did you really think that was true because that's wrong; you will get your ass kicked if you put that theory out there. That's not a good theory for you." He wanted me to come up with a theory to make something that everybody in my world would recognize as a non-fiduciary act—just a business decision basically—he wanted to make it something that was governed by the law we are experts in. I said, "Stanley, this is bogus. I came up with a couple ideas, but it won't work because of this. But I do think we have strong policy reasons that the law shouldn't apply."
>
> Rosa came up with a theory that would work, different from what Stanley wanted her to do.
>
> I walked into his office one day. A year before, we had told them this wouldn't work because of the way the law is. He crosses his arms across his chest and sticks out his fat fucking belly and says, "I just told the client that amending the plan was a fiduciary act, so JUST MAKE IT ONE." Oh yeah. "You did what?" I had to control my anger in a way that I've never had to control my anger in my life, because I wanted to kill him. He went off, and you could hear this man screaming at me up and down the hall.

Nobody, by the way, came to her aid while she was being screamed at. The fact that there are still work environments where shouting and insults are accepted is appalling to me. Sadly, I have heard these stories from many men and women.

From there on out, it was absolute torture for Rosa. She tried to avoid Stanley, or to defend herself:

> 'Stanley, I'm really trying to help you. You're going up against X and Y, and they are a huge law firm, and if you go up there without a way to support your point…' and he would yell and scream at me. I would sit there, and it was all in my stomach—the tension and stress. Meanwhile, I was building a practice. I had a national reputation even then—known nationwide. He used that situation as a reason to stop me from becoming a partner. Really? This is why he's going to stop me? Because he was wrong on the law and I wanted to help him?

As crazy as it sounds, there are people who will hurt themselves just because their egos won't let them accept advice—sometimes especially from a woman. And the more Rosa was right, the angrier Stanley became.

Gain strength from your goals

Rosa knew she had a war on her hands with Stanley, but she had her own goals. She wasn't going to let him—or anyone else—take her down.

> I never had to kowtow to the men. I had my own business [clients she had brought in that she was responsible for]. Most of the women didn't at that firm. I remember two women who were in my group; we

were all at a retreat, an all-partner retreat. And I was telling them some of my stories, and they were in horror that I would speak to some of the men like I did—because I didn't give a shit. One of them said, "You must have your own business," and I said, "Yes, I do. Don't you?" No. They called themselves "the maids," because they were basically maidens to the men that gave them business—beholden to them.

Rosa knew that she never wanted to be beholden to anyone for her business and needed to be able to speak her mind no matter to whom she was talking. "I didn't want to need them. My entire goal was to not need them. I didn't want to be a maid. I wanted to be powerful. But you can't be powerful in a firm unless people allow you to be powerful. I do not give power to men whom I don't respect." So Rosa kept fighting and kept building her own client base.

It is easy to get swallowed up in the drama of the workplace when you are facing opposition from others—or to be demoralized by the need to fight for what might rightfully be yours. Either can be exhausting. But you need to keep your own goals in mind and assess where each battle might take you in terms of meeting those goals. If winning the respect of a colleague or manager will lead you further in your career path, finding ways to do that is worthwhile. And if someone is placing obstacles in your path or making comments that might damage your reputation, you need to take action to protect yourself.

It could get ugly

Rosa stayed strong, focused on her goals, built her business, and felt free to speak her mind when she thought someone was wrong. That's why she remained a threat to the egos of some of her colleagues and perhaps a threat to the status quo, since many of the female partners got to be partners by being more agreeable.

> This happened when I was out on a retreat with my colleagues and other attorneys to discuss strategy. It was after dinner; we were having drinks. Stanley from across the table was having Sambuca. I said, "Oh, you know, it's that drink that all Latin American countries have, and they all taste the same." So Stanley says, "Hey, taste it," and I was getting close to him and saying that. He then looks over at me and says, "Why don't you go fuck yourself?," and it was at that moment I realized that they really were trying to kill me, and I was missing all the signs."

Another male partner in Rosa's group decided she needed coaching because she had "anger issues." She said, "Actually, I am angry. I'm really angry, Hank. I have really good reasons to be fucking furiously angry. I am rightfully mad."

"Well, you have to see a coach. Stanley is never going to apologize to you for telling you to go fuck yourself."

"Really."

"Oh yeah, he's never going to say he's sorry."

So she went to see the coach, and told her the stories of how she was being treated in her workplace by Stanley and others. The coach said, "It sounds like Stanley and Hank need a coach." As much as Stanley liked to scream at Rosa and others in the office, and Hank had equally unstable behavior—those actions were somehow accepted. When Rosa expressed her anger at being treated this way, she was sent to an anger management coach. Unfortunately, this double standard in the workplace is not unusual. Women are told to "calm down" or are seen as erratic or moody if they express any emotion at all.

Rosa saw that things were not going to improve for her, so she went out on her own after that, bringing her loyal clients with her. "I had been experiencing extreme shit for years and didn't realize it. I was a partner. I couldn't take it anymore."

Focus on what is important

To ensure she would be safe no matter who was against her or what tactics they used against her, Rosa had steadily developed a solid, long-term, satisfied client base.

> I have clients. The reason I am a lawyer today, and the reason I love the practice of law, is because in spite of these assholes who have been in my way, I have clients that adore me. They have been with me since 1998. The positive is, in spite of the tremendous obstacles I've encountered, I've had an incredible blessing—that lots of people have sought me out and stayed with me through all my moves. One client says, "Just show me the paper. I'll sign whatever you want. We're going with you." There's an incredible satisfaction in retaining clients for 15 to 20 years.

Be the best you can be

As much as I hate sports analogies, sometimes the best defense is a strong offense—not to start fights but to simply do a great job, bring the ball down the field. Opposition doesn't mean you can't continue to do good work. Satisfy your stakeholders. Do the right thing, consistently. Leverage your strengths. Improve your areas of weakness. Be excellent. Don't let the battle be all-consuming. Build a solid foundation to take with you if you find you have to move on.

Through all the turmoil, Rosa kept developing her business. On top of her billable requirements, she does 800 hours per year of non-billable, unpaid work. She gets on the phone with people, brings in new clients, writes articles, does speaking engagements. She wrote a book in her area of expertise and updates it regularly. She considers all this an investment in the business.

I asked Rosa why she was able to succeed. She responded,

> Let's not talk about what sets me apart, because it's not that simple. Some men will tell you they are set apart because they are brilliant, and it's total bullshit. At the end of the day, I just try to do the best job I can. I'm not always perfect. The reality is there are lots of complexities in the law. At some point you have to make a decision, and it's not always going to be perfect. It's as good as it gets right there for you, a point that lawyers will rarely admit to. Sometimes the answer is very black and white, and sometimes it isn't. So you have to make a calculated choice, and if you are going to be an effective lawyer, you give your client an answer. "Here's the answer. Here's your risk, your exposure, what we don't know." I try to give people an idea of the risk.
>
> There should not be anything unique about what I've just stated. It's how to approach the law.

At the end of the day, when we survive in spite of not having champions, we still manage to get clients.

But I'm not a fighter!

For some of us, learning to stand up for ourselves is a brand-new skill. We have been taught to go along, be passive, not make waves, and not complain. But make no mistake—if you don't stand up for yourself, nobody else will either. The more passive you are, the more you will be passed by. Whatever your upbringing, you need to learn *when, how,* and *why* to fight back.

When means choosing your battles wisely. Joe may have looked at you funny or made a joke at your expense, but complaining every time you perceive a slight will get you branded as a whiner and will make your real battles seem less important. Figuring out what is worth fighting for may take some trial and error on your part. Better yet, you can do some self-examination and determine where your personal lines are that you must defend. An off-color joke might not trigger you, but being repeatedly asked to clean up after the men at a meeting might make you feel subservient and is thus worth a confrontation.

How means choosing your weapons. Not every fight requires a full arsenal, but some do. If you go in with guns blazing, screaming "discrimination" and "lawsuit" at every sign of inequality, you will not only look ridiculous; you will also lose the respect of those who might otherwise support you. Bring only the weapon necessary to achieve the result you need.

What's needed may be a short note saying, "'Girly' is not going to work for me," without accusation, and the message is received: "Treat me with respect."

You may need to give a more strongly worded response or have a one-on-one conversation with the offender explaining what needs to change and why. Bringing others into the battle escalates its importance and the potential for embarrassment and defensiveness by the person you are accusing of bad behavior. Avoid this unless absolutely necessary, as it can bring unintended consequences.

If you are subjected to blatant discrimination or sexual harassment, you may need to escalate the battle. Bring in Human Resources, talk to your manager, or even consult the Equal Employment Opportunity Commission (EEOC) or an attorney.

Why do you need to fight? Because if you take only what is handed to you willingly, you will have a hard time reaching your goals.

Don't let the fight take away your personal power

No matter what is happening to you in the workplace, you come to it with your own strengths. You didn't get where you are by being weak. You've worked hard, studied hard, and paid your dues. To achieve the success you are reaching for, you need to become shrewder, and sometimes that requires fighting back.

Even as you are defending yourself, remember your strengths. Nothing anyone else does to you can take away your own personal power. Nurture it like a fire in your belly. Let the battle feed your flames instead of dousing them. You are worth it.

And if it gets to be too much, cradle that fire and bring it with you to somewhere that will allow you to grow and be your best self.

CHAPTER 9

PLAYING THE GAME

YOU KNOW OR ARE LEARNING how to fight for yourself when needed. You can scale your response to the battle at hand, using varying levels of strength. But what if you aren't up for a fight, or it really isn't worth it? How can you learn to play the game to get along and move up while still maintaining your dignity and self-respect? It's tricky, but it can be done.

Act like men

Some women feel they need to adopt stereotypically male behaviors and attitudes in order to work within the system—being more aggressive and less accommodating, for example. In many cases, being assertive is appropriate, especially when others are trying to take advantage of you. Rosa's strong, no-bullshit attitude may be more typical of men than women, but not everyone wants or needs to act that way to get what they want. Women have many strengths, and there are times to use them all.

A male friend of mine observed, "I always wondered if women in the workplace with powerful positions would eventually evolve into the men's seeing femininity as a strength and not just women showing masculine qualities." Would that it were so. . .

Play "cute" or "dumb"

As embarrassing as this may be to admit, at one time in our careers, some of us have either done this or watched other women do it. From our earliest years, we got the sense that boys liked us more when we were being cute and flirty and not so much when we acted smarter than they. Some women get into the habit of playing down their intelligence around men to make them more comfortable. Carrying that too far in the workplace, however, can be dangerous. If you are seen as too flirty or "girly," you may not be taken seriously, and you risk drawing the ire of other women, who know very well what you're doing.

As a young woman breaking into the computer/IT field, Valerie sometimes found herself being flirty with the men so they would be more comfortable around her. "I never had an affair and wouldn't sleep with the boss, but there are times when you feel you've got to be flirty and cute. Then you think, 'Oh, that felt awful, I don't want to do that.' Valerie learned there were other ways to get along, and as she matured and established herself in her career, she stopped playing that game.

Diana, Rosa, and Anne (all attorneys) had female colleagues who would be flirtatious, play dumb, and even have affairs with partners in an attempt to move up. Sometimes it would work—up to a point. The women would get promoted but still had no power. They had to continue to do the bidding of the men who helped them get there. They never gained the respect of the partners or their colleagues.

For the most part, avoid acting cute or dumb, as that can hurt your reputation and blunt your career trajectory. There are times, however, when these techniques can disarm a contentious situation.

Kowtow to the men

Really?

As bad as it sounds, some women are more comfortable in supportive roles and build their careers by helping men or other women succeed. The "maids" Rosa referred to in her law firm had moved up and even made partner by helping senior partners with their clients. The downside of this was that they had to do whatever they were told by the senior partners and never experienced the freedom Rosa enjoyed, because they didn't have their own clients.

Becky also saw that the new VP in her IT organization rewarded the "yes women," while he punished those who challenged him. In the long run, when the VP was fired, it is hard to say what happened to these women.

We all have to follow authority in our careers, and since many of our authority figures will likely be men, finding a way to cooperate with and help them to succeed is important. But you don't have to act subservient to simply respect authority.

Find what works with each person you encounter

Part of playing the game is figuring out what each person you work with needs—and providing that. Valerie discovered that many of the men working for her were encouraged by praise for their work or their brilliance, so she gives them what they need. In return, they are happy to help her with what she needs. She also found that the women she worked with were more interested in feedback and thanks on how hard they worked, so she gave that type of feedback to these women. Understanding the people around her and how to keep them happy has helped Valerie succeed, because her team is motivated and wants to please her as well.

Becky learned over time how to "manage up"—getting her manager to agree to what she wants:

> You have to learn how to manage up immediately. You will be more effective, because the boss knows what you are doing and why, and they are supportive. Someone asks me, "How did you get him to agree to that?" "Well, I went into his office and told him what I was doing and why he would want me to do it. What's the problem? Play to his strengths, and he will never tell you no if you give him reasons to tell you yes."

Asking your manager to do something he or she may not initially want to can take some courage, but the rewards can be great. If you are confident in your abilities and believe what you are asking for is the right thing, there is no reason not to seek it out.

Shirley, a former human resources director in a large defense contractor, also recommends figuring out what each person needs and using that to learn to work with them. She provided this advice frequently to employees who would come to her with issues dealing with one of their managers or coworkers—sometimes with specific suggestions based on what she knew of the manager. "Bill is very busy, and he likes to hear just the overview or highlights of what you are doing. Don't bog him down with the details; it just annoys him." Or, "Joe is very detail-oriented, so be prepared to answer a lot of questions about your project."

The best way to figure out how to work with specific people is to pay attention. Watch how they talk, whom they seem to enjoy being around, the types of interactions that work well, and those that don't. Everyone is different, but few people are so complex or difficult that you can't find ways to work together successfully.

Prepare—then present your case

The more you understand about the people you work with, the better you will be able to influence them to help you. Give them what they need, and they will return the favor.

The same applies to the overall organization. Know what the mission is and try to tie your goals into that mission. Pay attention at the company meetings to the long-term and strategic goals. Give serious thought to how your work can positively contribute to the company strategy and absolute priorities. Practice articulating that. "If I take this approach, I can help reduce the time to market for this product by four weeks."

Presenting a suggestion tied closely to your manager's or organizational goals is extremely powerful. Successful women use this technique to present their ideas and advance their careers.

Use humor to defuse awkward situations

Sometimes the best thing to do is laugh. Reacting to every situation as if it's the most important thing in the world will get you labeled as uptight or worse. Often it's better to just find the humor in the situation or make a joke to relieve the tension.

Missy, as the youngest person and only female salesperson in her company, is often asked to pick up lunch for meetings. Annoyed that she is the only one tasked with that, she tries a humorous response,

"Let me check the chore wheel. Oh, look, it's Joe's turn to pick up lunch!"

Make it their idea

Sometimes we learn this strategy through trial and error and frustration. We suggest an idea in a meeting, get a friendly but dismissive nod, and are ignored. A little while later, someone else (usually a man) suggests the same thing in a slightly different way, and everyone jumps on it like it's the best thing since sliced bread. This can be extremely frustrating, but it can also be used to your advantage.

If you really want your idea to be adopted and expect pushback if it comes from you, you can play the game. You must first accept that you may not get credit for your idea, so only use this if you are willing to forgo attribution. Seek out someone who can put forth the idea and be accepted. You can either directly ask that they promote your cause as their own or make subtle suggestions about what you would like and see if they will bite. Then when they suggest it in a meeting, you can jump on it with all your support. "That works!" Some people are so skilled at doing this that the person who presents the idea in the end comes to believe it was theirs in the first place. The difficult part about this approach is that you probably won't get credit, and it can feel demeaning to feed your ideas to someone else.

Try amplification

If it rankles too much to let others take credit for your ideas, perhaps the women in the office can support each other. In a *Washington Post* article in September 2016,[6] reporter Juliet Eilperin reported on a strategy adopted by women in the White House during the Obama administration.

Frustrated by being ignored in meetings, "Female staffers adopted a meeting strategy they called 'amplification': When a woman made a key point, other women would repeat it, giving credit to its author. This forced the men in the room to recognize the contribution—and denied them the chance to claim the idea as their own.

"'We just started doing it, and made a purpose of doing it. It was an everyday thing,' said one former Obama aide who requested anonymity to speak frankly. Obama noticed, she and others said, and began calling more often on women and junior aides."

Since the article came out in September, women in Washington and other communities decided to adopt the approach, banding together to support each other in their workplaces. If you work closely with other women and have problems getting your voices heard and acknowledged, consider talking with them to see if this approach will work for you. Having colleagues on your side when you put forth ideas certainly can't hurt.

Make it their choice

Karen, an HR director for an automotive group, has a unique way of getting people to do things they don't want to do. Rather than insisting they *must* do something, when they start to push back on her, she tells them they have a choice. According to Karen, "If I say, 'You have to do this,' it's different than if I say, 'It's your choice. I'll explain to you the consequences of your choices.'

---

6   Eilperin, Juliet. "White House women want to be in the room where it happens." WashingtonPost.com. https://www.washingtonpost.com/news/powerpost/wp/2016/09/13/white-house-women-are-now-in-the-room-where-it-happens/ (accessed October 17, 2019).

"I had someone ask me, 'Do I have to fill out this form?'

"'No, you won't get short-term disability if you don't fill it out, but you don't *have* to.'

"'Well, I better fill out the form.'

"'Well, it's your choice—if that's the choice you want to make.'"

Somehow, this is more acceptable than insisting someone fill in the form.

Karen, a master of the game

In Karen's role as HR director for the male-dominated automotive sales group, she runs into many situations where she is challenging long-held traditions and culture—by the nature of her job, she is a threat to the status quo. She uses all the techniques at her disposal to gain the cooperation of those she is trying to change.

Welcome to the car business

Karen's background was in HR for government contracting organizations, where there were plenty of challenges but nothing like what she saw once she joined the automotive group. Two days after starting her job, she was called by one of the managers at a dealership to investigate a sexual harassment claim. She arrived with her manager, planning to watch and see how things were done in the company. When they pulled into the dealership, the salesmen who were standing around outside laughing together looked up, suddenly alert and trained to seek out the potential customer. When they recognized Susan, the head of HR, they relaxed a little and then watched as Karen approached, clearly curious who this new person was. Karen and Susan said "Hello," then headed inside to interview the manager of the dealership and the young lady with the complaint.

They sat in the manager's office and waited while he brought in the young woman. She walked in looking a little jittery, eyes looking at Karen and Susan and then away as she took a seat. She was young, maybe twenty, smooth, dark hair pulled back into a low ponytail, slim except for the bulging belly she seemed to be protecting, arms wrapped around and cradling it with her small hands. Susan smiled at her reassuringly.

"June, I understand you had a problem here. Can you tell us what happened?"

June looked up at her manager, face reddening, and stammered, "Well, John over in Sales said something that made me uncomfortable. He's done it before, you know." She looked back down at her hands, caressing her belly, and gave a little shudder.

Karen took in the situation, and then asked the manager to step outside and give them some privacy. She leaned forward to the pregnant girl, and asked, "To the best of your recollection, can you tell me exactly the words that he said?"

June's face reddened more deeply, and she wrapped her arms around her chest. Then her brow furrowed as she brought back the exact words. "He asked me, 'When are you going to get milk in your boobs?' And then he said, 'Oh, don't worry about it. I'll see when you have spots on your shirt—then I'll know.'" June's eyes filled, and she rocked in her chair a little as she said it. She looked away.

"Thank you for telling us," Susan said to her. "It was right to bring this to our attention. We will take it from here." Karen left to speak to the manager, while Susan stayed to talk further with June.

When Karen walked outside, she found the general manager and CEO laughing together. The general manager was making light of the situation. "Oh, *sexual harassment!* He doesn't mean anything by it. He's just being funny. You know John's one of our top salesmen, right? He's been with the company for years." The CEO nodded. "I know. Good guy—maybe not the smartest, but you know how these things are." The two of them shook their heads a little, smiling.

Karen interrupted. "You know you could lose your dealership over that, right?"

The men stopped smiling and looked at her.

"You have someone under 21 spoken to by a man in that manner. You know about it; I know about it. You have to do something." She turned to the CEO. "And I'm not referring to just this one store. You could lose your whole dealership over this. If you want to do battle for this guy and risk your whole dealership, that's your business, but you need to know what you are risking."

The CEO swallowed hard and glared at Karen. "Uh, I need to fire him?"

"Yeah, you need to fire him," Karen responded. Two days into her new job, she was threatening the status quo. It would not be the last time.

Karen did the right thing, even though she was risking the ire of her new CEO. She didn't stomp her feet or insist on firing the employee. She just calmly explained the risk he was taking by keeping him on and let him decide. Just a few days into the job, she could have been intimidated and taken a softer stance or laughed it off with the rest of them—but she held to her principles and the responsibility of her job in HR to advise management on these issues.

Soon after that, she had to fire a long-term employee who was surfing pornography on the showroom floor with his back to customers, so customers could see what he was looking at when they walked by.

I thought this was not the way we wanted to be. It's me that has to make the firing decision, because they would say "Oh, he's been with us for years; he's always done that." What I would do is explain the business implications: "Okay, so the customer walks by and sees that. What if there is a child with them that sees that and they take you to court? You are going to lose, because everyone in the company knows he does that, so you are creating that business implication and also putting yourself at risk for a lawsuit. Over something like that, you're going to lose. There is no high ground here."

Choose your battles

Karen needed to take a stand on the important issues, and she did so carefully and methodically, explaining the implications of the decisions being made. But she had to learn to let some things go, to give a little. The language she encountered with the men in the field was shocking compared to the government contracting environment she came from—but she knew not to try to change too much. "I won't let them say racial or sexual things to each other. I'm taking away a lot of natural things they do, but I'm not going to take away their swear words. That's the unholy balance we've reached, and that seems to be fine with everyone."

Just as Karen has decided some things are not worth fighting for in the larger scheme of things, you too must decide when to fight back and when to let things go. Part of playing the game is being flexible.

Non-confrontational solutions

Karen knew she needed to add value to the organization beyond being the sheriff of the employees' bad behavior. She brought in a human resources information system (HRIS) to help track vacation and other leave. Then she needed to get the employees to enter their information into the system and fill out forms they didn't want to bother with.

> My boss said (not to me, but to someone else— I heard about it) that we were light years ahead in HR from when I started, using the HRIS. She wondered how I did it. If I had gone in saying, "This is the way we have to do it - my way or the highway," it never would have worked—especially as a woman getting these men to change their ways.
>
> There was a gentleman who didn't want to use the new system. I sat down to explain to him how to do it, and he started attacking me. "Every other HR department I've worked with can do this. Why can't you do it?" It was a personal attack, and there was a big part of me that wanted to say, "Every other person in this company gets this. What are you, stupid? What's wrong with you?" I have a pretty nasty temper, but I've learned over the years how to recognize and control it, so instead, I said, "I'm going to step away from this meeting and let you guys finish up." My boss and he were still in the meeting. "I think I've said all I can say." I left, and his boss later called me to say, "I'm so sorry. I can't believe he was talking about you like that."

Karen's decision to walk away from the meeting rather than responding in anger was a wise one. An angry confrontation would not have resulted in change, and she was able to maintain the high road and the respect of her boss.

Karen received two kinds of pushback when she needed people to change how they were doing things: direct refusal to cooperate and passive-aggressive response: "Here's an old form. I used a crayon with information I think you want. So you can log in to fill it in for me." Karen would respond, "I could do it, but security doesn't work on the system to allow me to."

With some folks, she used the "It's your choice" technique, or she would say, "Why don't you try this? Open up your program; click on this button; do this; do this." One of the general managers said, "That's it? Why haven't I been doing this before?" Rather than confronting and insisting people follow her direction, she would gently guide them until they were able to see the value in what she was asking.

Sometimes you have to say "No"

More precisely, Karen saves times of confrontation for when they are necessary and effective. There comes a point where you have to say "No."

> There was a guy in one of our vehicles who pulled up into our lot on a group of our employees, pulled out a handgun, pointed it at them, and said, "Drop your pants, boys; there's a new sheriff in town." The employees all laughed. His manager called me and said, "This is what happened. What do you think?" Again it was another long-term employee. I said, "I

think you should get the boss on the phone and tell him I'm on my way down there, because if you don't take care of this, I will."

"Well, uh . . ."

"Let me see if I understand correctly: our vehicle, our property, our employees."

"Well, the gun was empty."

"I don't care. And what if it wasn't?"

So I went down there and I fired him. You've given me no choice. You pick your battles. Sometimes you walk away from things that are not the best thing. They are not illegal, not going to hurt the company but not the best decision. I sometimes walk away from those. But when it's going to hurt the company, that's my battle and where I'm going to stand. They don't like it.

They are a good group and didn't want to fire that man. They wished he hadn't done it. He was a good employee. But the manager understood. We grieved the choice the employee made and the choice that it left with us, but we had to say goodbye.

When it's important enough, you have to stand your ground, even against the opposition of others.

Games people play

Karen knows she needs to help her employees improve, and she needs to get cooperation from those uninterested in change. To do this, she needs to use all the techniques described above. "I spend a lot of time saying, 'You're so smart, so tall' to feed the egos of men and women. Otherwise I'd be totally ineffective. I need to build them up so when I have to have them do something, they'll listen. I'm not dishonest about it. There is always something good to say about anyone."

Karen watches people and sees that many women are dumbing it down to keep from being a threat to men. She does the same as needed. "You can't be the smartest person in the room. I do a lot of feeding others an idea and hoping they repeat it, so I can pounce on it and say, 'That's a great idea.'"

Karen also uses humor to lighten the mood in tense situations.

> I have an employee who was frustrated with his employees in a dealership. He yelled out, "I work with a bunch of dicks." So his employees thought it would be very funny to draw pictures and put it on his monitor and on his chair. I got a call from the manager, who said, "It's not harassment, because it's two males doing it to another male." Okay, let's go through this again. He kept saying, "I don't get it, don't understand where you are coming from." Finally, I said, "It's not against the law to be a dick. It is, however, against the law to draw pictures of dicks and put them on someone else's computer." He sat there, started kind of chuckling, and said, "Well, if you want to put it that way." I try to be gentle, try other methods, then boil it down to something a little off-color—funny—but in the end I say, "You have to do this. This is going to hurt the company." I have to go through the steps.

If Karen just came in like a bull in a china shop and tried to lay down the law all the time, she would see less cooperation from her

YOU HAVE WHAT IT TAKES

coworkers and the people in the dealerships. She has found many ways to stay likable and fun despite her job of making people toe the line.

> I use humor to keep you off-guard, so I can slide things in—not in a cruel way—if I could get you to laugh. In my mother's eyes, if you are funny, you can stick around. So I use that around the boss. We sit and laugh a lot. First: life is short. Second: if he can see me on a human basis, I can get more stuff done. Early on, someone said, "I'm not in this for the money, just for the sheer entertainment value." Some of the things I've run across, I'm in it for the entertainment value.

Use your words

During her time with the automotive group, Karen has run into many situations where the language used is not something she would normally be comfortable saying. But she knows she needs to parrot those words sometimes to get people to admit what they have said.

> Sometimes I have to practice. I interview the employees and find out what he's been saying, and then I have to go home and practice those words. I'm not a lamb, but I certainly don't use some of those words. I would never call a woman that word. I have to practice. If you're the manager, I always ask your side of the story—and find it's always sanitized. Then I'll just do a direct quote: "So, you didn't ask your employee how their fuck-fest was this

weekend?" We'd been there 15–20 minutes, and I've been Miss HR. It's funny to see the shock on their face. "Why don't you just tell me what really happened?" They've been given a clue, I already know. But there have been times I've had to practice those words—nice to have a husband at home to whom you can walk in and say, "Guess what the word of the week is?"

After the shock, they come around and drop their barriers. "Here's the thing: If you continue down this road, you will be fired. I guarantee that, because the company is going to be sued, and I'm not going to allow that to happen—if I have to choose between the company and you, if you don't have other words you can use with your employees. First of all, don't talk to them about their personal lives. What do you care what he did this weekend?"

And I'll give them words to use. One salesman I overheard say, "Man, that guy is retarded." I'd stop them and say, "We don't use that word anymore. Let's use *developmentally disabled* or don't use it at all. Why? Because it offends." You give them a different word and hope they will use it.

It never hurts to be nice

We all want to work with people we like. We don't always get the choice of how others act, but we can certainly put in the effort to be likable ourselves. Karen was coaching one of the managers in her group, trying to get her to be more helpful and cooperative with employees.

She was rude to people. Someone would call to tell her their health insurance was declined, and her immediate and terse response was "Call the insurance company, I don't know why you're calling me." We're overhead. You need to make yourself valuable. You have to be nicer.... We received complaint after complaint. One day the CEO said to me, "You know, I just don't like that woman." This was a problem. I had to call her in and give her awful corrective action, detailing times and dates on when she said what to whom. I bought a box of Kleenex. We needed them. The next day, a new person walked into work. She was perfectly capable of being nice and helpful; she just never did it. Only when her job was on the line did she listen to my coaching.

Part of playing the game is to be gracious and helpful even when you feel frustrated or overloaded. This is something most women can do naturally, but if you find yourself snapping more than helping, consider what that might be doing to your reputation and your career. Savvy women find ways to get along with their coworkers and managers.

Pulling out the Bitch hat

On the flip side, there are times when things need to be done, and you may have to be more forceful than nice. Karen tells her new employees during the interview process:

> "Don't be fooled. I am a bitch. We have goals, and
> we need to get them done. I want you to know that.
> I may be nice to you now—I'm recruiting you. It's

okay. I have a job I need to get done, and if I have to be a bitch to do it, I will." But that's a word they use to try to hurt your feelings. I'll say, "I have a hat in my desk with a big old B on it. You want me to get out my Bitch hat?" And a boss will say to me, "I think you need to get out your B hat for this one." So they recognize they are responsible—we can do it the nice way, or I have a hat in my drawer we can do it the hard way.

Karen's technique, while not for everyone, has the advantage of bringing humor into the situation and also defuses the dreaded B word. The sentiment behind it, though, applies to all of us. Sometimes you need to be firm, and you need to let people know they have the choice of doing it the hard way or the easy way.

Remember, it's just a game

I am a competitive person. I love playing games, and I love to win. Once a year, I get together for a vacation with my mom and a couple of her friends, and we play bridge a lot while enjoying the beach or other area attractions. As retirees, they play bridge several times a week. I play once a year. You can imagine how often I win. But the beauty of bridge—or any other game—is that after each hand, you shuffle cards and deal out another hand. I get satisfaction from a single hand bid and played well and try not to think about what the cumulative score would look like if we were to add it all up. Along the way, I learn new tricks and strategies that I can use in the next hand. I am improving.

Each day we go to work, we have an opportunity to look at the hand we've been dealt and figure out how we want to bid and play.

Sometimes the cards are not in our favor, and we just have to get through the day with as little damage as possible. Other days we have great cards, but our opponents are especially shrewd, and we don't do as well as we should. And other days we are at the top of our game, and we prevail no matter what comes at us. Each day we learn something new is a good day.

You can approach your career as a war—or as a game. Shift your perspective. Reframe it. You will face a series of challenges, small advances, setbacks, hands won and lost, strategies developed and executed. You can have fun along the way, and you will undoubtedly be frustrated by some of the obstacles you encounter, but each day is a new opportunity. Watch those around you. See what is working for them. Learn what makes your boss tick. Mimic those who are finding success. Use all your strengths and some or all of these strategies. Above all, be savvy when that means playing your way to success.

CHAPTER 10

CHANGING THE GAME

SOMETIMES, NO MATTER how much you fight back or learn to play the game, you can reach a point where you know there's no way to win. The obstacles are too great. Then you can either beat your head against the wall, give in, *or* you can find a way to change the game.

The other possibility is that you really take stock of where you are in your life, question your career direction, and ask yourself if you have lost your passion for your chosen field . . . and realize there is something you want to do that's more appealing. Nothing says you have to stay in the line of work you chose when you began your career path. The point is, sometimes you have to make a big move—either to stay or go. Then, with careful thought and planning, you change the game you are playing.

Open up to possibilities

Changing the game can include everything from asking your boss for a different assignment to moving to a different group or job within your organization, quitting and moving to a different company, or even changing career paths or starting your own company. Very few people move straight up the ladder in a single organization these days. You have to make your career work for you, and if something is in your way, you need to find a way around it.

Often we are prompted to make a change through sheer frustration. Becky, the IT marketing director we discussed in Chapter Six, fought back against her new VP when she was being treated unfairly—until she realized the fight was futile, and she took her talents elsewhere. Rosa, the fiery attorney from Chapter Eight, built up her client base so that she would be free to change law firms when fighting back no longer worked for her. Valerie, when faced with a manager who demoted her because she wouldn't sleep with him, quickly started looking for another job and propelled herself forward over her career from computer operator to vice president of IT at a large insurance company.

All of the women represented in this book have taken detours in our paths, changing the game as needed when fighting back or playing along no longer made sense. I personally have changed jobs within a company, changed companies, and even changed my choice of career paths on more than one occasion. Quite likely you have done this yourself—or you will at some point. It is up to you to decide when enough is enough and to make the changes necessary to *keep your life moving forward.*

Where is your passion leading you?

Sometimes the motivation for change is less about an obstacle or battle you are fighting and more about something pulling you in a different direction. Perhaps you are exposed to a new aspect of your field that feels like a better fit for your interests and talents. Pay attention to where your passion is leading you—because you will undoubtedly be better at a job you are passionate about than one you find boring or disagreeable.

When you were young, you might have been exposed to a few occupations, and when asked what you wanted to be when you grew up, chances are you said "teacher," "doctor," or "president" if you were especially ambitious. Later, as you learned more in school and perhaps chose a major in college, you may have thought you had it figured out. *This* is what I want to do. Many of us find once we enter the workplace, however, that very few jobs resemble exactly what we learned about in school and that there is a wide world full of interesting and challenging work opportunities. Don't limit yourself to what you knew when you were 6, or 18 . . . or 50. You can *always* change the game.

Looking within your company

The first thing you can try if you are in an area that is not working for you is to see if there is an opportunity to change jobs within your company. When I was working for a satellite company writing test plans, I felt like I had a dead-end job, and I wanted something more interesting. I volunteered to help the Marketing group represent our services at a couple trade shows, and talked more extensively to them about what the job entailed. That's when I was first exposed to technical marketing and applications engineering—jobs that could use both my technical and people skills. I wanted to move my career in a different direction, and my company had positions that looked more appealing to me. I spoke to my manager about making the move to Applications Engineering, and he wouldn't allow it. He said I was too valuable in writing the test plans (which I found boring and completely unchallenging). Meanwhile, I was getting medio-cre reviews in the Test Engineering position—and realized it was because I was not passionate about the work. Ultimately, I ended up leaving that company for a new one, making the career transition I wanted but with a new company.

Convincing management at your company to allow you to move to a different position, perhaps in a different group, can be challenging, especially if you are a valued employee. Your current manager may not want to let you go. You may need to do some creative convincing to help make it happen: outline a transition plan while they backfill your position, identify someone else in your group who could be groomed for your position, or get the new manager to fight for you.

As a last resort, and only after you have secured another position elsewhere, you can make it known that you need and want to make a move . . . or you will have to leave. Be prepared to accept "No" for an answer and make the move, as many companies don't take well to ultimatums.

Changing companies

Loyalty is something of an old-fashioned concept, at least when it comes to your career. The days of working 40 years for the same company and then retiring are all but gone. The average employee changes jobs every 4.6 years, on average, according to Bureau of Labor Statistics data from 2012. Younger people change jobs more often, possibly as they are finding their way to a career that fits. Depending on the field, the average may be higher or lower than that. It's generally a good idea to stay within the average range for your field, or you risk being branded as a job hopper. But generally speaking, if it's not working for you, you don't have to stay. It's as simple as that.

The bonus is that you can often increase your salary dramatically, get a promotion, or move into a job or company with more upward mobility. You can also get an ego boost just by fleshing out your resume and reminding yourself how amazing and talented and productive you really are.

Changing careers

When your passion is pushing you in a different direction, you may decide to change your career path completely. Similarly, if you find you really hate what you do or have conflicting feelings about where it is leading you, you may need to consider a larger change. This is a lot riskier than just changing jobs within your field, but it can be incredibly rewarding. To reduce risk, do your homework. Figure out what is needed to break into the new field: more schooling, specialized training, connections? Research the salary levels to see what impact this will have on your life. Look at the time commitments in comparison to your existing career and make sure it will work for you. Involve your family and friends as needed in the decision process, especially if it will impact their lives or lifestyle.

Once you understand as much as possible what you are getting into, then go for it. Don't let fear stop you from seeking your own long-term happiness.

Opening your own business

Many women these days are finding success in opening their own businesses. Women own 36% of all businesses, according to the 2012 U.S. Census—a jump of 30% over 2007. According to entrepreneur.com, women own 10.6 million businesses in the United States. They employ 19.1 million workers—that's one in every seven employees. Their businesses account for $2.5 trillion in sales. According to the 2015 Kauffman Index: Startup Activity,[7] women entrepreneurs are more adept than their male counterparts at seeing gaps in the market and seizing the opportunity.

If you have an entrepreneurial spirit, and the hard-work ethic to go with it, you may want to change the game by opening up your own business. As always, research and understand as much as possible about what you are getting into before making the leap.

Shirley, an HR professional playing the game

Shirley built her career in HR at a huge defense contractor, playing the game for over 20 years and moving up to the top 1% in a 100,000-person company. She learned and used all the techniques for getting along—becoming quite well-connected in her environment.

The corporate culture in this defense contractor was built around deference to the mostly male, mostly ex-military executives. HR was considered a support staff function, and though mostly staffed by women, the leaders in the early days were men. Shirley learned early on that to get along with these men and achieve success, she needed to play their game.

"I played a 'little woman' role—supporting the men, being deferential. If I was cute and flirtatious, they didn't see me as a threat, and they liked being around me. I learned the lingo and acronyms, talked their talk, and pretended to care about the things they cared

---

7   Fairlie, Robert W., Arnobio Morelix, E.J. Reedy, and Joshua Russell. "The 2015 Kauffman Index: Startup Activity; National Trends." Kauffman.org. http://www.kauffman.org/~/media/kauffman_org/research%20reports%20and%20covers/2015/05/kauffman_index_startup_activity_national_trends_2015.pdf (accessed October 17, 2019).

about. These men were former generals and captains in the military, used to getting their way."

Shirley parlayed her ability to get along with others into movement up the career ladder. She was young and attractive, and she learned to use that to her advantage. She played cute but never dumb. She earned the respect of her peers and managers, as well as that of the employees she was representing in her HR role.

An introvert in an extroverted world

As an introvert working with mostly extroverted leaders, Shirley had to find a way for her voice to be heard. She was not always comfortable speaking up at meetings. That became even more difficult once she realized that her original ideas would not get adopted if she proposed them herself. If a man later suggested the same thing, even repeating her idea verbatim, everyone would agree what a great idea it was. Eventually, she stifled herself in the meetings, going along to get along.

Her introverted personality worked to her advantage, however, as she was able to carefully study and understand the people around her. Instead of talking all the time, she was listening and watching. Her insights into what each person needed were spot on. She found that if she took the time to craft her ideas and suggestions into an email, she was able to make a much larger impact.

If you are also an introvert among extroverts, find ways to have your voice be heard. If you are more comfortable formulating your thoughts offline and submitting them via email, that is always a better option than stifling yourself. (Writing your idea in an email also creates a record of whose idea it was in the first place.) You may also find it easier to share your ideas one on one with members of a group rather than in large meetings. Remember that introverts tend to have deep understanding of the situation and people involved—use this to your advantage. Successful women find ways to achieve their goals using their unique strengths.

Teaching others to play

In her HR role, Shirley was called on to advise others how to get along and fit into the corporate culture. Often women would come to her frustrated with the male-dominated, my-way-or-the-highway culture. With her years of experience in the company, Shirley knew there was little chance of changing the culture. She tried to help the women understand that.

"The system is bigger than you or me. You have a choice. Can you accept this and get what you want within this corporate culture?"

Because Shirley had studied and understood the various managers and employees she worked with, she could give specific and helpful advice—how to play the game:

> Joe is busy and thinks on a high level. He likes it when you are short and to the point. George is still an engineer at heart, and he wants to really dig in and understand the details. You need to give him more specifics, or he will think you don't know what you are doing. Yes, Jack is all arrogance and bluster, but he is your boss. You need to show him respect and stroke his ego. Feed him ideas that he can use to talk about how great he is to his management. You may feel like you aren't getting credit for your ideas, but Jack knows who is helping and who is not.

Not everyone Shirley advised could work in this environment. Feeding ideas to someone else felt wrong. Stroking someone's ego for the purpose of getting ahead felt disingenuous—even if the compliments were true. Shirley recognized that some women would be unable to tolerate this kind of strategy—or at least not for long. For those women, she encouraged them to consider changing companies or moving to a different group. She could see that they would continue to be unhappy with the existing corporate culture.

The people Shirley worked with liked her because she gave them good advice for getting along in the company. Her management liked her because she understood them, gave them what they wanted, and didn't make waves. She moved around within the company, establishing solid relationships . . . and slowly making her way up the chain to the top 1% of employees.

Taking stock

If you find you are uncomfortable playing the game, stop and take a good look at what is troubling you. Do you feel like your personal integrity is being compromised by doing what the company is asking of you? Does your conscience bother you when you think about the mission for your work or the way you are treating others in your job? How difficult is it for you to support a manager who treats his or her employees poorly?

Our first instinct may be to find a way to get along in our job and to get ahead. Sometimes, though, you need to honor what is intrinsic to your character. If your job requires you to compromise on your core beliefs, it can wear you down to the point you don't know what you believe any more. Take care that this doesn't happen to you. If you feel it happening, find a way to change the game.

The slow burn

Shirley played the game well and achieved great success in her company. But something was wrong—something she ignored for years until she couldn't any more: She was faking it. She pretended to be passionate about her company and her industry. She played along with the idea that defense contractors were providing the tools to save the country from its enemies. She knew that was true—but in her heart she was a pacifist. Outside of work, she became involved with social activist groups protesting war.

She pretended to like her management team while abhorring their management style and treatment of their employees—especially women. She endured being ignored and humiliated. Once when out at a field site, the new CEO showed up to meet with the team. She was the only woman, and everyone else was former Navy brass. The CEO chatted it up with everyone, feet up on the table, then leaned back and said, "Let's go out and get some beers." They all got up to head out, and the CEO literally slammed the door in her face as if she weren't there.

She watched women get stuck at the mid to senior level in her company, and she pretended that was okay. She saw smart, capable women who couldn't even get to the director level.

She endured one boss who screamed at her, excluded her from important meetings, and told her he didn't trust her. He was dismissive, abusive, unwilling to listen, and clearly didn't like women. Her company thought that was just fine.

She pretended to care if the company she worked for was profitable. All the corporate meetings at her level were focused on profit and financial growth rather than leadership or taking care of people. She wanted more. As she got older, she started examining who she was and what she wanted from life. She realized her chosen career was sucking the life from her, yet she felt trapped by the success she had achieved.

Finding your core

If you find yourself feeling this way in your work, take the time to examine what is behind it. Are you faking it? If so, why? Is there a misalignment of your core values with your company's, or even your choice of career? You may need to make some changes.

If you have lost sight of your inner beliefs along the way or have never really thought about them, there are resources available to help you figure this out. Books such as *Discovering Your Authentic Core Values: A Step-by-Step Guide*[8] walk you through determining what is important to you. Your own discomfort with where you are can be a wake-up call that you are in misalignment.

Once you determine what is wrong and what you need, you will need to figure out how to get where you need to be. A course correction to bring you closer to your personal values in your career path is critical to your happiness and success.

The final straw

While Shirley had embarked on a new spiritual path outside work, she encountered a serious obstacle in her job. She was by then the head of HR for a 15,000-person sector, which due to a reorganization was merged with another large sector. Shirley had a long professional relationship with the vice president of the newly formed sector, and she was very highly regarded by him and his management team. Joanne, the HR lead from the other sector, had less experience and fewer connections in the new organization, but she was given the role as Shirley's manager. She considered Shirley—with her experience, knowledge, and strong connections—a threat, and she launched many tactics against her.

8   Schelske, Marc Alan. (Portland: Live210 Media, 2012).

Joanne put Shirley in the middle of a conflict between Joanne and the VP with no authority to resolve it. She withheld critical information, making Shirley look bad. Suddenly Shirley was left off the think tank teams that were critical to knowing what was going on and influencing the direction of the organization. Clearly, Joanne did not want Shirley to succeed. "I felt like I had a target on my back," Shirley says.

Then Joanne started telling Shirley, "Your peers are concerned about you." When Shirley asked who, Joanne would not answer. "Your peers say your heart is not in it." But she wouldn't tell her who said these things.

"It was crazy-making. All those years of hearing nothing but glowing feedback about my performance, and suddenly I'm told my peers are disappointed with me. With no knowledge of where this was coming from, there was nothing I could do about it."

Shirley couldn't take it anymore. She took a good hard look at herself and her career, and she realized it was no longer right for her. Perhaps it never had been. She needed to stay true to herself, in spite of the costs of walking away from a company, career, and six-figure salary.

Shirley left her company and started seeking a new career path that was more in line with her personality and belief system. It was time for her to change the game. She knew that the longer she stayed in, the harder she would find it to realign her job with her core values.

Sometimes it's time to throw open all the windows and doors and be open to any new direction—even if it isn't a linear move ahead on the same path you were on. Sometimes you may REALLY need to change the game . . . and sometimes you just need to play it somewhere else. Maybe you just need to work with a different team of people, who respect and support each other. Being with great people can make all the difference in job/career satisfaction even if the money isn't as great as where you were.

Staying true to yourself

Most people find they need to compromise on some of their ideals once they enter the workplace. Very few people have the luxury of working in a perfect job with perfect coworkers and management. Most of us have worked with annoying coworkers, endured ridiculous behavior from management, or had to do things that were boring or unfulfilling, at least for a while. Masterful women learn to play the game to get along as needed, but they also recognize when the game is no longer right for them and they need to change it.

At the heart of the decision to move on is self-knowledge. What do you truly want? What is your personality type, and does it fit with your job? Does your company hold a different belief system or have a culture that tolerates behavior you find intolerable? How much can you live with?

When changing companies, you need to understand what you are getting into. Many companies now put their mission statement and core values on their website. Read them and see if you are in alignment. If you can't find them, ask during the interview process. Even if the company mission and values are similar to yours, watch and listen carefully to how the people you are interviewing with act. Some companies screen out people who don't align with their values but not all. Once you are on board, continue to pay attention, making sure the people you are working with are ones you can trust and get along with. If you stay true to yourself, you are much more likely to be happy and successful in your work.

CHAPTER 11

STAYING PROFESSIONAL UNDER FIRE

SOMETIMES, EVEN WHEN you do everything right, shit happens. You find yourself in an untenable situation. How do you keep your cool when things fall apart around you?

Accomplished women learn to navigate through bad situations with dignity. This is not easy, but it's worth it.

Connie: From dental hygienist to marketing project director

Connie started her career as a Dental Hygienist back in the Seventies and Eighties, when dentists were primarily male, and the hygienists and other staff were typically female. Though Connie worked in some offices where the dentist—and boss—was supportive of his female staff, there were others where that was not the case.

Dr. Maxwell, the older man we met in Chapter Two who had a string of ex-wives and a temperament to explain it, ran a tight ship.

When Connie, after cleaning and examining a patient, suggested to the dentist that Mrs. Wilcox had decay in teeth 4 and 16, Dr. Maxwell brusquely took the instrument from her and leaned over the patient, muttering, "I'll be the judge of that." Connie sighed and stepped back, quietly taking notes as the doctor called out during the exam, "Number 4 and Number 16, cavities." Connie felt her frustration at being treated like an inferior, unintelligent *girl* by Dr. Maxwell mounting, and so she did the smart thing and started looking for something else. She needed to change the game.

Time for a change

George, a young environmental engineer, had formed a company to develop safety programs for doctors and dentists, but he had no experience with implementing safety procedures in a medical setting. Connie answered an ad requesting a dental hygienist familiar with the rules and safety procedures and happily joined forces with George. Connie now had the opportunity to use her skills and experience in a collaborative, entrepreneurial environment.

Suddenly, Connie found her intelligence and work experience valued as she taught George what he needed to know about dental practices and risks. At the same time, George taught Connie about the business, and they grew the company together in a truly collaborative environment. She started taking business classes to increase her knowledge and skill set, working toward her MBA. Over time, she and George hired a sales force, managed by Paul, an entrepreneur who partnered with George in the company.

When Paul eventually forced George out, he kept Connie on, because he valued her knowledge and contributions to the business. She was promoted to vice president. After her years of working under dismissive and domineering dentists, Connie was finally using her skills and business acumen in an environment where she was valued. After a satisfying day at work, she went home to her family each night excited and energized. Could this be true? And could it last? Connie had successfully taken a risk, changed her career trajectory, and was on a new path forward.

When you are contemplating a career move, you need to carefully evaluate how the change will impact your life. Is the new job a backward step in pay or position? If so, you may need to find a way to make up the difference, at least for the short term. You may also be taking a risk that you will be successful in the new career. You can't always know if your skills or temperament will fit until you try it.

To minimize the risk, research as much as you can about the potential job or career. What do you need to do to build your skill set to be successful in the new position? Connie knew that to move from dental hygienist to working in the business world, she needed a different education. She went back to school for her MBA part time while working in her new company. She found she could immediately apply what she was learning on the job.

Once you have figured out what you need, evaluated the risks, and taken the necessary steps to smooth your path—just do it. Don't let the thought of having to shuffle around the deck chairs of your life keep you from jumping ship to another workplace or career path. Never just stay stuck.

The new guy with an old attitude

Connie had become a key player in her company, and she loved it. When the company needed additional money to expand, they brought in venture capitalists for funding. A condition of their investment was that they would bring on a safety expert, Jack.

When Jack arrived at the office the first day, he did not act like "the new guy." He eyed the size of his office relative to Paul's and Connie's, and only briefly returned Connie's handshake when she introduced herself, turning quickly to give Paul a hearty greeting, complete with a clap on the back. Paul told Jack, "You will be doing work similar to what Connie has been doing, and so she will work closely with you to bring you up to speed. Feel free to ask her any questions you have along the way." Paul's eyes widened quickly then narrowed as he turned back to Connie with a tight smile. "Well, I guess we will be working together then." Connie smiled back and got right to business. "Why don't you get settled in, then join me in my office, and I'll go over some things with you. I'm sure you'll fit right in."

Connie was eager to share her knowledge and to share the load of the work she was doing with Jack. She and Paul were welcoming and helpful as Jack learned the business. Sales were increasing, and the company was poised for growth—all part of the plan when they brought in the additional funding. She didn't see the disaster ahead of her.

Disparaged

The first time Jack screamed at Connie, they were alone in her office going over a report he had prepared. Connie pointed out a section where he had made a mistaken assumption, and provided the background on why it was incorrect. As she spoke, Jack's face turned beet red, until he slammed his hand down on the desk and shouted, "What the hell do you know? You're just a woman." He snatched the report and stomped out of the office.

Connie sat there immobile, processing what he had said to her. *What happened to the team environment? Who the hell does this guy think he is? Doesn't he know I'm just trying to help? And that it's important to get these reports right if we want to retain our clients?* She took a deep breath and tried to rationalize it. *Probably he's just having a bad day. He's never done this before. Let's just wait and see how things go.*

Soon Jack's verbal abuse became a pattern. He belittled her in private and in front of coworkers, tearing apart her arguments and telling her she was stupid. She fought back where doing so was warranted, when she was sure the facts were on her side and it was important to get them right. She tried to dismiss his rude comments and refocus on the work at hand, but his hostility was wearing her down.

Sometimes she felt like she was under Dr. Maxwell's rule again—in an atmosphere that was abusive, domineering, and evidenced no respect for women. Still, Connie kept her cool. She still felt that Paul was on her side, and no matter what Jack said, she knew when she was right. She tried to ignore his comments, realizing that the behavior was Jack's problem and not hers.

Staying professional when encountering abusive behavior in the workplace is one of the hardest things to do. But getting into a yelling match with a colleague is not going to help anyone. When Becky was yelled at by a manager early in her career, she walked away from him, saying she would continue the conversation when he had calmed down. If you can successfully get away from the abuser, that may be the best way to maintain your composure. For Connie, however, the situation was escalating.

Dismissed

On the day of the big client meeting, when Paul, Connie, and Jack would be presenting their safety program to the customer, Connie dressed in her sharpest black suit and heels. She strode into the conference room, greeted the clients with a smile and a firm handshake, and took her seat at the table. Connie had been in charge of this project, and as she began to introduce it to the client, Jack interrupted her by sliding a pad of paper and pen in front of her. "Here you go, Connie," he said with a smile. "How about you take notes? I'll take it from here." With that he turned toward the customer, presenting Connie with the back of his head as he spoke, while she sat fuming. He leaned in to the lead client and whispered loudly, "She's been such a big help on this project, but I'm sure you'd rather hear about it from me, right?" The client looked confused, having worked with Connie for months on the project and knowing she had spearheaded the effort, but Jack was already into the spiel, so he let it go.

Disheartened

Not wanting to make a scene in front of the customer, Connie pushed the pad of paper aside and shifted her chair away from Jack. She listened to him present her report, lips pressed tightly together and hands clenched on the table in front of her. When he misspoke about one of the safety procedures, she interrupted him to correct him.

"Actually, Jack, if you'll recall, that particular process won't work. Instead we recommend using this newer procedure to better protect against contamination." The client looked at Connie to hear more, but Jack again dismissed her with a wave. "Now, Connie, it's all here in the report. I'm sure Joe here can read it for himself." Connie sat back, mouth agape, as he moved on to another section of the report. She looked at Paul for support, but he just sat there looking at his hands, twisting a pen and avoiding her stare.

And undefended

After the meeting, Connie marched into Paul's office. "What the hell was that? Are you going to let him get away with that crap?" Paul looked up, eyebrows knitted together. "Now, Connie, calm down. It's not that bad. Jack is just showing off a little. It's just Jack. Everyone knows how he is. You need to get a thicker skin."

"Are you kidding me?" Connie paced back and forth in front of Paul's desk, too keyed up to sit.

"We all know you did the work. And you know the venture capitalists want Jack here and involved. There's nothing to be done about it, so you just need to learn to live with it." Paul's words were like a punch in her gut. She was clearly going to get no help from him, after all those years of working together to grow the company.

Unable to respond, Connie turned on her heel and walked out, shutting herself into her office to think. *What was going on with Jack? Why did he suddenly have it in for her? He wasn't treating the other women in the office poorly . . . but they were not in the position she had. Was he threatened by her? Did he see her intelligence, experience, and history with the company as getting in the way of his success?* His behavior made no sense. Connie didn't have any problem with helping Jack learn, and as far as she was concerned, the more people knew and contributed, the better for the company as a whole. Clearly, Jack didn't feel the same way, and he seemed determined to take her down.

Almost more disturbing than Jack's behavior, though, was the lack of support she felt from Paul. She and Paul had been a team before, working together to build up the company even after George left. She couldn't believe his response to Jack's public insults. *Was he really going to let Jack get away with this? Did he have no loyalty to me after all these years? "Get over it"? Really?* Swallowing hard against

YOU HAVE WHAT IT TAKES

the lump in her throat, Connie picked up the next client's report and got back to work.

Keeping emotion out of it

Many women would have a hard time staying strong when faced with a situation like Connie's. To hear a colleague ask, "What do you know? You're just a woman" would make me incredibly angry—justifiably so. It most definitely made Connie angry. But if she had reacted in anger, Jack would have known he had gotten to her. Bullies love upsetting their victims. Connie didn't want to give him the satisfaction.

More importantly, Connie didn't want to risk her job or career by crying or yelling in front of Jack or Paul. She didn't want to be labeled as "an emotional woman." And she was too much of a professional to call Paul out or make a scene in front of a customer.

So what do you do with the justifiable emotions that come from this environment and behavior? Many of the women I interviewed have encountered tough situations, and we all have tried to keep our cool—with varying degrees of success. Judy advises bringing a bottle of water into a potentially difficult meeting. If you feel an urge to cry, take a drink. Look up at the ceiling—that is supposed to keep you from crying. Excuse yourself and go to the bathroom or outside, where you can let it out and then regain your composure. Find someone outside of work to vent to and potentially get advice from about how to handle the situation. Figure out what your next move is going to be. Having a long-term plan can help you tolerate bad situations in the short term.

The end game

As Jack's abuse escalated, and Paul did nothing to stop it, Connie knew the end was near for her. She did her work, fought back when Jack was especially cruel or especially wrong, and waited for the axe to fall. When her parents came to visit after her father's prostate cancer diagnosis, Connie decided to take a couple days off to spend with them. She was cooking breakfast when Paul called her that Friday, asking her to come into the office. She refused at first, reminding him that she had previously planned this time off, but when he insisted, she agreed to meet him there at 1:00.

Here it comes, she thought as she exited the elevator and headed for Paul's office. When she entered, he looked up at her with pained eyes, as if his dog had just died. She pursed her lips. "What's so important that you had to drag me in here on my day off?"

Paul gestured for the chair across from him. "Please, sit down, Connie." She sat, looking at him expectantly, her face blank, giving him nothing. She was not going to make this easy for him.

Paul started to ramble. "Connie, you know how important you are to me, and to the company. You've done so much to make us the success we are. You know that, right?"

Connie looked at him. Nodded. Said nothing. Waited.

"I have always been able to count on you," Paul continued. "We were a team, and we worked together so well all these years."

Connie noticed the past tense, but kept quiet.

He continued to list her accomplishments, while she waited for the "but." He spoke about Jack, how the venture capital firm really wanted him in that position, and how much Paul appreciated Connie's helping Jack to get up to speed when he came on board. Eventually he spoke about how Jack and Connie "didn't get along," somehow making it sound like it was her fault that Jack screamed insults at her and demeaned her in front of the customers. He was squirming and nervous. He talked straight for an hour and a half.

Connie sat quietly and looked at him, face blank.

Paul finally said it: "Connie, I hate to do this, but it's out of my control. I'm going to have to let you go."

When Connie said nothing, Paul kept talking, eyes beseeching her. "You know how much I care about you."

This is starting to sound personal, Connie thought. She said nothing.

"Connie, you know I've been vicariously in love with you."

Connie stared at him, lips clamped together and thoughts spinning through her head. *How dare you? This is how you're firing me—by telling me you're in love with me? By telling me how you felt our relationship was? We were collaborative; you could count on me. Meanwhile, you don't have my back when someone is abusive to me— what a great partner you turned out to be.*

She stood up to leave, still saying nothing. Paul stood and walked around the desk toward her. "I'm so sorry, Connie," he pleaded, reaching for her. "Can I have a hug?"

Connie turned and walked out of the office. She suddenly felt powerful to be able to just reject him and walk out. *Yes, emasculate him right as he exposes himself.*

Exit with dignity

As bad as things got for her, and as ridiculous as her final meeting with Paul was, Connie kept her dignity all the way to the end. She didn't give Jack or Paul the satisfaction of seeing her emotions. As torn up as she was inside, she held her head high and walked away.

I often wonder if I handled it correctly; I chose to say nothing and let him struggle with what to say. It wasn't that I was afraid to argue some issues with him. I was just so *done* with all of the crap, and I must admit I enjoyed watching him struggle with his words when I knew exactly what he was going to say. I was angry that, after what I had done to help him build the business, he did not have my back when there was a very abusive person who came into the company.

Being let go from a job—whether through a layoff or firing—is a huge blow to the ego. It can cause all sorts of emotions, from sadness to shock to anger and despair. It can make you want to lash out at those responsible, to take others down with you.

Don't do it. Keep your cool. Walk away and deal with the shock later. Emotional responses will just convince the people letting you go that they made the right decision. Don't give them the satisfaction.

Picking herself up

Connie had changed the game by moving from Dr. Maxwell's oppressive dental office to a collaborative work environment, and in the process, increased her skills and confidence and experience. When the game changed again for her, she found herself back in an abusive and oppressive situation, but she was not the same person she was before. She had helped build the company and was confident in her abilities. She fought back.

Even in losing, though, she found the win. Connie's years of helping to build up the company with George and later Paul had helped her realize her own value, and she wasn't going to let Jack take that away from her, even as she lost her job. She took her skills to a medical market research company—run by women. Once again, she was in a collaborative team environment where her expertise and experience were valued. Connie became a senior project director and was a key player there for many years until her recent retirement.

Keeping your cool through it all

Sometimes we do everything right, and things still go badly for us. There are no guarantees. Companies have layoffs. Management changes, and you find yourself working for someone you can't stand—or who can't stand you. You make a calculated career change and find the environment untenable.

It is easy to sink into self-pity or to blame yourself for moving from the frying pan into the fire. It is easy to question your self-worth when you are let go, even if half the company is down-sized. It is easy to become paralyzed with fear—what if I make another bad move?

Savvy women keep going, one decision at a time. *If this decision doesn't work out, I'll make another one.*

Savvy women keep their cool. *This really, really sucks, but I am not going to lose it. If I can get through this day, I can go home and cry and come back tomorrow. My career is too important, and this person giving me grief doesn't deserve the satisfaction of taking me down.*

Savvy women find the win—even in the midst of losing. *I may be losing this job, but I gained some excellent experience I can take with me to a company more deserving of my talents.*

Be savvy. Find your win. Keep your cool. Keep going.

CHAPTER 12

NEVER GIVE UP

THERE IS NO ONE SOLUTION or tactic that works for everyone in all situations. Most of us have to try different approaches depending on what is happening. The more experience, knowledge, and street smarts you have, the better you will be able to choose the appropriate response to your current challenge. But you may find you need to change, adapt, and try different strategies to see what will work, abandoning those that don't. Sometimes, you have to try everything.

Like many smart women who are used to succeeding, I was not prepared for the people who were determined to stop me. I expected that I would be competing on a level playing field with other men and women, and that I would succeed or fail based on my own merit. I hadn't figured out yet that I was a threat: to my manager's ego or to the status quo. And I didn't consider that being a working mother would be used against me.

Early success

At first, I believed I had beaten the system. After all, I stayed in the workforce, got my master's degree, and got promoted to manager of a 20-person Engineering Department at the relatively young age of 29—all while raising my two children. Perhaps there was no glass ceiling after all, and even being a mother was not going to get in the way. I didn't realize that my head was touching that ceiling already—and I'm only 5 foot 3.

I had jumped into managing the Engineering Department with gusto. I held monthly department meetings, bringing in donuts and updating the team on what was happening in the company and on their projects. They voiced their concerns, and I brought them to upper management with suggestions for improvement. I drafted memos about office moves and even proposed a reorganization that better aligned projects with their managers. I coached my employees and had five young engineers start work on their master's degrees with my encouragement and example. I wrote proposals to bring in new business and keep my department fully employed. Meanwhile, I continued to be program manager and lead system engineer on two programs, including the multimillion-dollar hardware test system I had proposed and designed over the years. The thrill that went through me in the morning as I drove to work about what was coming each day allayed any misgivings I may have had about leaving my children with the babysitter. My job was using all my skills—technical, people, presentation, writing—and all of my brain. I knew my strengths and was leveraging them. In short, I was on fire.

Playing the game

Perhaps I was oblivious to some of what was happening in my company. In a way, that may have been a blessing. Assuming my opinions would be listened to and my talents valued, I gave it my all. As much as it is important to understand the world around you, sometimes it is better to assume the best of people so you are motivated to put forth your own personal best. I ignored the insulting comments and unequal treatment of women in my company. I went along to get along.

Seizing the opportunity

Powerful women always bring their best to work so they can feel good about their contributions and look at themselves in the mirror at the end of the day. When the opportunity came to be promoted to the next level, I jumped at it. It was just a baby step up, really, as deputy to the director who was currently above me—a new position created to groom the person who would ultimately become the director. I wanted it. Even more, I believed I would be excellent in that role. I put my name in the hat.

I was one of only two candidates for the job. The other was my office mate, David, who managed the Software Engineering Department. He was smart, funny, and good at his job. On paper, we didn't look that different. David had maybe one more year of experience; I had a master's degree he didn't have. We had similar positions within the company. I never had trouble competing with others—men or women—in school, and I wasn't worried about it now. Game on.

Juggling priorities

The morning of my interview with Dick, I put on my best dark blue power suit and a white blouse. I even managed to tie a scarf attractively at my neckline—I hadn't quite let go of the eighties. Panty hose and sensible pumps completed the look. I hoisted the baby on my hip, diaper bag and brief case hanging from my shoulder, and ushered the kids to the car for daycare drop-off. The thrill of excitement running through me reminded me of being in college, heading off to take a final exam knowing I had studied hard and was bringing my best to the test.

As difficult as it can be to juggle the demands of home and work, the payoffs can be enormous. Figure out what you want and then find a way to get it. I loved my children, and I loved my work. The balance of the two responsibilities used different parts of my mind and heart. I was confident I could continue to grow in my career while raising my children—with the help of daycare and my husband.

The deputy director interview

At 10:00 a.m. exactly, I walked from my office next door to Dick's office, shoulders back and head high with a wide smile. *I've got this.* Dick was sitting at his desk, facing the right-side wall, looking at his computer. To my right, behind him, was the open door to Tina's former office. Tina had been his budget analyst who had recently quit to raise her daughter.

As soon as I was seated, he threw me a softball question, "Why do you think you are qualified for this position?" I answered confidently, reminding him of my accomplishments in proposal writing and managing my team. My limbs were loose and relaxed, and I gestured freely as I spoke. I talked about my vision for the Special Projects Group and how I looked forward to working with him more closely as we moved toward that. He listened carefully, nodded as I discussed my vision, and even jotted down a note.

"Why do you think you are more qualified than David for this job?" A fair question, though the fluttering in my stomach reminded me this was not an easy one. He held his gaze steady. My hands fidgeted in my lap for a moment, then stilled as I found my answer.

"David would also be an excellent choice; there is no question of that. But my experience in writing the winning proposal, leading the design effort, and managing the XLNT program is much more complex than the projects David has worked on. I have done that while managing the Engineering Department at the same time. I have a master's degree in engineering that David does not have, and five of the engineers on my team have followed my guidance and example to pursue their own graduate degrees. I would bring this experience and education to this position, and I am confident we can work together well to continue to grow this group."

Comfortable with this response, I smiled and relaxed a little, sat back in the chair. Dick's expression tightened just a bit, and I watched him carefully as he pondered his next question. "How do you propose to manage your workload with these new responsibilities?"

That was another fair question, which I had already prepared for in advance. I told him how I could delegate more of the responsibilities in the Engineering Group to Chris, my deputy department manager, and suggested that Bill was ready to take on more of the project management tasks for XLNT. I would still oversee everything and represent the program with the customer but wouldn't need to run the daily project meetings or code reviews. This was completely doable. I leaned forward, hands gesturing as I spoke.

Preparation is key

I had prepared for the interview knowing I was up against a solid candidate. I reviewed my up-to-date resume, reminding myself of my accomplishments. I went through my past performance evaluations—solidifying my belief that I was doing great and would fit well in this position. I knew how my skills stacked up against David's and was prepared to answer honestly if asked about that. All of this gave me confidence and the ability to respond quickly to Dick's questions.

Any time you are facing an internal or external interview, you need to take the time in advance to review yourself. Know your strengths and weaknesses. Be prepared to play up your strengths. Also be prepared to discuss your weaknesses—almost all interviewers ask about that, and an honest answer is better than pretending you are perfect. If possible, learn about the other candidates and figure out what differentiates you from them. You can either address this directly or find ways to put forth your strengths that you believe position you better than others. I had prepared well for the interview.

A curve ball

I could see in Dick's face he wasn't expecting this response to managing my workload. His brow furrowed as I spoke, and he fidgeted and looked away, planting a seed of doubt in my mind. *What was wrong with that?* I wondered. Dick paused and took another tack, mouth turned down. "What happens if a proposal comes up and you need to work late?"

I eyed him a moment, trying to figure out where this was going. He knew my schedule and that I typically worked 8 to 5 every day, leaving to go pick up the kids after work. He also knew I had worked plenty of proposals late into the evenings when it was necessary. I reminded him of that, my mouth now a thin line. I spoke slowly, carefully. "Of course, if I need to work late, I will do that, just as I have in the past." My stomach fluttered a little thinking about my kids, but this was just hypothetical at this point anyway. My hands twisted in my lap, and I worked to keep my face calm.

Dick looked away as I spoke, dismissing my words with the side of his face. I held my breath, waiting for what was coming. He continued to push: "Okay, so what happens if you are in a meeting with a customer, and it runs late, and you can't leave at 5:00. It's last minute, you hadn't planned on it, but it's absolutely necessary that you stay."

My breath came out in a rush. *What the hell? Why is he asking me this? When does this ever happen? What exactly does he have in mind for this job? Is it going to be a 60-hour workweek? He never said anything about this before.* My mind raced to figure him out and determine how to answer this ridiculous question. I tried not to think about what it would do to my family if I were to suddenly have to work long hours. I shook the thoughts out of my head and responded calmly, my teeth slightly clenched, "I would call my husband and ask him to pick up the kids, then stay and do the work that is required of me." *Did I project an angry tone? Is he hearing anger or desperation in my voice?* I would need to watch that.

The gut punch

In spite of my efforts, Dick seemed to notice that he was getting to me, and he leaned in for the kill. "What if your husband is not available to pick up the kids?" Suddenly I knew what he was asking. He wanted me to choose between work and my kids. He was not going to let me have it all. Anger flashed through me. He had no children and no compassion for their needs or for mine. *How can he ask that of me? How can I abandon my children for my own selfish ambition?* I gripped my hands together in my lap to keep from reaching up to twist my hair. My cheeks reddened, and I felt the telltale burning in the back of my nose. *Damn it.* I was going to cry. There was no stopping it.

I slumped back in my chair, face screwed up against my will and tears running freely now. Stomach quivering, I made my choice. I looked up at Dick with a sinking feeling in my chest and told him, "I will have to think about this and get back to you."

I saw the victory in his eyes and the small smile on his lips, even as he brought his brows together to project a look of concern. He handed me a tissue and said, "Of course. You just let me know."

As I stood to leave, thoughts careened through my brain as I quickly made my way down the hall to the bathroom, head down and nose dripping, hoping nobody else would see this. *I am pathetic. Hopeless. I can't even get through an interview without breaking down in tears. I don't deserve to be promoted. Dick is right. What was I thinking?*

Losing it

I knew better than to cry at the office. I didn't always keep my cool. I knew it showed me as weak, emotional. Apparently Dick knew it, too. I felt like he purposely pushed me in that direction, until I couldn't help it.

I should have excused myself earlier, when I could feel myself losing it—or looked up at the ceiling, which I'm told now prevents you from crying. Or brought a bottle of water in with me to take a drink and compose myself. Or, I don't know, punched him instead of crying. Okay, not that.

The fact is, I lost it. It happens. It wasn't the first time, and it wasn't the last, though I have learned to control myself or my environment enough to where it doesn't happen anymore now.

If you happen to get emotional—to cry or get angry at work—know that you are not alone. It is not ideal, but you can recover from it. Forgive yourself; then take the time out to calm down and refocus on your goals.

After I had composed myself in the bathroom, I returned to my shared office with David with just enough energy left to flop down into my chair. He looked up with a smile, "How did it go?" I shrugged and asked casually, "Did he ask you about your ability to work crazy long hours at a moment's notice?"

David laughed. "Of course not. Why would that be necessary? It's a job that doesn't even exist today. Why would it need that?" I rolled my eyes and laughed along, masking the anger that suddenly shot through me, replacing the despair. "Good point, David. Good point." I needed to forgive myself and figure out a way to recover. What helped me to do that was my anger.

Time to fight back

Whether I had run into the glass ceiling or the "Mommy wall," clearly I was not going to move up any further without a fight, and I couldn't fight without the support of my husband. This promotion would mean more money for our family, and if we wanted it, he would have to step up and take on more responsibility at home. I spoke with my husband that evening, and he agreed to be available for the kids if I needed to work late occasionally. This also opened up the conversation about roles and responsibilities, and we worked out a schedule for drop-offs and pickups that was both fair and flexible. This was going to work.

The next morning, I squared my shoulders and marched into Dick's office, though my stomach was quivering. He looked up and jumped a little when he saw the look in my eyes. "Have a seat," he offered, gesturing to the chair across from him.

"No, thank you. I'll stand." I leaned forward with a smile, placing my hands on the back of the chair. With a strong, clear voice I told him, "I spoke to Randy last night, and we are going to make some adjustments at home. He is very willing to step in and help more." I watched Dick squirm in his seat, looking away from me as I spoke. "I am willing and able to put in the hours necessary to do this job, and I don't want that to be a consideration on whether I get the promotion."

The room was silent. I didn't say another word, waiting for his response. Dick's eyes traveled over his desk as if looking for something, and he tapped his pen on the table. I watched and waited. Finally, he looked up with me, a pained look on his face, shaking his head. He spoke quietly and deliberately, "I don't doubt your sincerity . . . but I'm going to have to think about it."

I gripped the back of the chair to keep my knees from buckling and clenched my teeth. *He doesn't doubt my sincerity? He doesn't believe me! He has already decided he wants David and is using this as an excuse.* I forced myself to release the chair, put on a smile, and say it again. "I am willing to work as hard as necessary to do a great job for you. I hope you will consider that." I turned and walked out before he could say anything else, fists clenched by my side.

There was no doubt in my mind now that Dick was not going to choose me for the position, and he was justifying it by tilting the playing field, so the ball rolled in David's direction. I have no problem losing to someone who is better than I am, if I am evaluated fairly on my merits. But in this case, my motherhood status was being held against me. Never mind that David had three children at home—his wife was home caring for them. Dick never even asked David about his ability to stay late during his interview, yet he grilled me about mine. David had even reminded me—this was a brand-new position. How could it require more than full time?

Escalating the fight

I did not get where I was by giving up easily. My five brothers taught me to stand up for myself, and I was used to competing success-fully in school. I was not going down without a fight. If you have no success with your manager, you can move your fight up the chain. I made an appointment with Doug, the vice president and Dick's boss.

Doug had hired me straight out of college nearly ten years before, and I felt like we had grown up together. He had moved up from Engineering Department manager (my job now), through director and on to vice president, adding a few gray hairs with each move. He was friendly and smart, his body short and stocky—look-ing a little like Fred Flintstone but with the personality of a smarter Barney Rubble. He had no children, but he had a lovely wife I had met at company picnics and Christmas parties. Doug had always been supportive of me in my career, helping me move from engineer to program manager to department manager. Though he was now two levels above me, he felt like family, and I was sure he would have my back.

As I walked to Doug's corner office in the front of the building, I thought about what had happened with Dick, and the heat rose in my face again. I set my shoulders, took a deep breath, and strode into the office. Doug's office was long and narrow, and his desk was at the far end. He looked up and smiled, reminding me of our years of comfortable friendship, and ushered me over to the round table closer to the door I was standing in.

As he walked over to join me, he saw the look on my face, and his smile turned more serious, kind eyes questioning. "What can I do for you, Mary Ellen? Are your kids okay?"

Immediately with the mention of my children, my mind quickly went back to their small faces, and I lost my focus for a moment. Then I remembered and steeled myself. "This is business. I need to talk with you about the deputy director position."

We both sat down, the round table making me feel more collegial and collaborative than I did sitting across from Dick the day before. But without the table between us, I felt more exposed, and I tugged my skirt down a little as it rode up over my knees. I decided not to cross my legs.

Doug jumped in right away. "Well, you know that Dick is the one making that decision, right?" He looked at me, then quickly away, leaning back in his chair a little.

Coward. My resolve only got stronger.

I leaned toward him, resting my left arm on the table and gesturing with my right. "That's what I wanted to talk about, actually. In my interview with Dick, he pushed me pretty hard on my ability to stay late at a moment's notice."

Doug's brow wrinkled a little, as he thought about that.

"I'm embarrassed to say he kept pushing until I felt like he was making me choose between work and the kids, and I ended up crying." It was all I could do to keep from feeling like crying again as I thought about making that choice. I decided anger was safer, especially when I saw Doug looking away from me. I curled my toes inside my pumps, pushing down until it hurt, while keeping my face and voice calm.

"I went home and spoke to Randy, and he agreed to do more of the daycare pickups and be flexible as needed for situations that required me to stay late. When I told Dick about it, he said he 'didn't doubt my sincerity,' but I could see that he didn't believe me."

I paused and looked for Doug's reaction, holding my breath. He was looking around the room. I waited. He shrugged a little, then looked up at me. "What do you want me to do about it?"

He didn't get it. I could see that he did not understand my indignation. "What was the problem here?" he seemed to project. I let out a long breath, then said "I want my availability to not be a consideration in determining whether I get this promotion. I am telling you that I am dedicated and willing to do the work required, and that it would not be fair for this to be held against me." Okay, so the anger was starting to creep into my voice. Tough shit.

The blatantly illegal question

Doug looked straight at me, his face blank. "Let me ask you this, Mary Ellen. Do you look on this job as your career, or are you going to quit and stay home with your kids?"

That hit me like a brick in the chest. *What the hell? How can he even ask that? I brought my baby in here on my MATERNITY LEAVE to support acceptance testing. I nursed her in the conference room, for God's sake! You don't get a more dedicated employee than that.* I tried to breathe, to think of a reasonable response to this completely unreasonable—and illegal—question.

I sputtered, "Yes, of course I do. I work hard, care about this company. You have seen how hard I worked to get my master's degree, how much I've put into my career here." I was frantic, grasping at answers. "Why would I want to toss that aside?"

His face was cold, hard. He sat back, put on a casual smile. "Well, Tina did that, and I know you are friends, so I was just wondering if you were considering it." Yes, Tina, who had worked her way up in the company from receptionist to budget analyst and had been there for over ten years, had quit to raise her daughter. But I was not Tina. I completely respected her choice, but it was not mine.

My mouth formed a thin line, and I responded through gritted teeth. "No, I am not going to do that. But you know, anyone can leave a company at any time for other reasons than to care for their children. Have you asked David if he looks on this job as a career?"

Doug could see now that my anger was directed at him, and perhaps he recognized that he had crossed a line. He smiled reassuringly, "Well, I'm glad to hear of your dedication to the company. I'll talk to Dick if you want, but I'm sure he will be fair."

He stood up, reached his hand out for a handshake. I was being dismissed. I looked at him with disbelief and caught myself before giving him a piece of my mind. I shook his hand perfunctorily, gave a tight smile, and said, "Thank you. I do hope so," before ushering myself out the door.

As I walked back to my office, I tried to keep the angry energy moving me forward. I tried not to think about the betrayal I felt, not just from Dick but also from Doug—Doug, who had known me for years and whom I had looked up to since I was a newly minted college graduate. I couldn't believe it. By the time I reached my office, I knew that I was not done fighting. This was no longer business—it *felt* personal.

I had not yet learned that sometimes business is business–that no matter what type of personal relationships you have outside of work, they don't always apply during office hours. As painful as this was, I now believe that Dick and Doug liked me as a person and would happily hang out with me at the company picnic. They just didn't see me—a woman—as the same caliber as the men working for them. That is the crux of the problem.

Knowing the law

I was not an attorney. But I knew enough to know what had just happened was borderline illegal, if not completely so. After all, this was the era of diversity training, where companies brought in experts to teach their employees about the law and how to treat each other.

I had gone to the diversity training classes with the rest of the company, crowded into a conference room for hours on end watching videos and listening to lectures about sexual harassment, affirmative action, and equal opportunity. I kept my mouth shut when I overheard some of my male colleagues complaining afterward that HR was just trying to cramp their style. Personally, I thought their "style" could use a little cramping, after years of watching Henry giving back rubs to the women in Publications while I was trying to get them to finish a proposal I was working on. After years of feeling like I was "too sensitive" when I was offended by the sexist comments going around the office, it was nice to feel validated and supported. And since they had hired a diversity manager in Human Resources, they seemed to be eager to make the work environment more comfortable for women and minorities, providing us the same opportunities for growth that our white male colleagues enjoyed.

After my conversations with Dick and Doug, I wanted to see how serious my company was about these issues. I made an appointment with HR.

Finally, someone on my side

Darlene was a tall, big-boned woman with impeccable hair and makeup at all times. She had a real presence, striding through the halls in her colorful yet polished suits and high heels. In her role as diversity manager in Human Resources in a company dominated by men, with a few women mostly in lower-level positions, she had her work cut out for her. Women adored her; men feared her.

Her office on the first floor was small but welcoming, and I shut the door behind me when I entered. As I sat across from her, Darlene could tell by the look on my face that things were not okay.

"What can I do for you, Mary Ellen?" Her wrinkled brow and concerned eyes gave me the freedom I needed to tell my story. The tightness in my chest released a little.

As I told of my first visit to Dick, her face tightened and lips pursed. When I got to the part about crying, she reached over to pat my hand and said "Now, now. We all lose it sometimes." But I could see she was angry and sensed it was not with me. When I told her that David wasn't asked the same questions, she let out her breath in a huff and sat back hard in her chair. I went on, and when she heard Dick's "I don't doubt your sincerity," she leaned forward and said, "Are you kidding me?"

When I told her I had gone to see Doug, she smiled—until I got to the part where Doug asked if I was planning to stay home with the kids. Then her face went blank.

I sat back, relieved of my story, and waited while Darlene took it all in. Employment laws had already been violated in several ways, and she had to make the call between protecting the company and protecting the employee. Darlene tapped her pen on the desk, shifted in her seat, and let out her breath in a huff. Suddenly she smacked her hand down on the desk, startling me, and leaned forward. "All right, here's what we're gonna do. That shit cannot happen in this company on my watch."

Relief flooded me in a rush, and I smiled at her determination. "Dick and Doug are required to file paperwork with HR before any promotions, and if there is a protected class in the mix (women, in this case), they will need to justify choosing a man instead—if they choose David, that is." She went on from there, but I just sat back and smiled, knowing that she was going to make sure this was a fair fight. It's all I ever asked for.

Using Human Resources

If you run into an issue with your employer, as I mentioned before, a good first step is often to talk with someone in HR. Technically, they are supposed to be the employees' advocate. However, the situation can be tricky if you are reporting something that could put the company at risk. The HR representative may be in the position of choosing whether to support you or reduce risk to the company. You may find they first try to talk you out of being upset—minimize the damage. If that happens, listen carefully and try to be honest with yourself: are you overreacting, or are they are underreacting?

But a good HR person will work to both support you and reduce risk to the company, helping the employee by working with the employer to make necessary changes. Perhaps they need to have a conversation with management about what is happening and how that might impact the company. As discussed in Chapter Nine, Karen found herself in that position many times working in HR for an automotive group.

HR cannot be effective in instituting positive change if they don't know about the problems. Too many people wait for their exit interview to tell about all the issues with a company, when it is too late for them to benefit from any changes.

The end run

Two days after I spoke to Darlene, at 5:00 p.m., Dick called my office. He was offsite but wanted to let me know that he had chosen David for the job. He had already notified David and the other managers of his decision. "It was a difficult choice, but I have decided to go with David for deputy director. Thank you for applying."

My heart sank into my stomach, but at least it was over. "I'm sure David will do a great job," I sputtered before hanging up. Suddenly the urgent project I was working on didn't feel so urgent, and I packed up my things to go home.

The next morning, I stopped by Darlene's office. "Hey, I guess you heard they chose David for the position," I told her casually, leaning against the doorway. "They must have had some good justification, I guess."

Darlene stood up suddenly. "What? How do you know they have chosen David?"

I was confused. "Dick called me last night. Said he told David and the others about it. I figured you knew. He would have had to do the paperwork, right?"

Darlene's face darkened, and her hands went to her hips. "No, he did not submit the justification to HR yet. I would have challenged him to review it. I've looked over your performance reviews, and they are stellar. They even mention how you are running the largest department and the largest contract in the group." Exasperated, she continued, "He decided to go around HR and announce the promotion before we got involved, so it would be too late. Unbelievable." She sat down hard.

Her anger was contagious, but she was right: it was too late. No way would we overturn the decision now that everyone knew. Dick had gamed us all and won. As she prattled on about how she was going to make them answer for their actions, I knew it was hopeless. They would come up with their justification somehow, and it's not like David wasn't qualified.

Trying to change the game

I had worked hard and given my company my best. I had played their game, ignoring the male-dominated culture and pretending that only my contributions mattered, not my gender. I prepared for the battle—shoring up my defenses to handle the hard questions about my capabilities. I underestimated my opponent—Dick—and, in a moment of weakness, let him get past my armor. I shored myself up and went back in fighting. I escalated when needed and brought in reinforcements from HR.

But Dick outsmarted us, and I lost the battle. Darlene was convinced I could still gain something, and that Dick would need to make up for his deceit. We tried to change the game.

She insisted management identify the "gaps" in my experience that made David the better candidate in their eyes and then make them agree to put me on a fast track to fill those gaps. After all, I had been with the company for nearly ten years, and if I hadn't been given the same opportunities as David in areas that were important for advancement, that too needed to be corrected.

Too little, too late

I was glad to know that someone in HR had my back, but in the end, none of it mattered. My blinders were off, and suddenly I could see the subtle and not-so-subtle behaviors that created an environment where women's contributions were not valued as highly as men's.

The new org chart came out with David's name under the deputy position, with mine still as department manager with 20 engineers under me. (David had 15.) I noticed again the "Technical Staff" block, reporting directly to Dick, with the names of engineers who were pulled out of my group when they promoted me a few years back. This included Joey, who I had discovered was making more than me years before with less experience, education, and responsibility, and who presumably still was, or else why was he not in my department? There were no other women with any sort of authority in the entire SEG and only one other that I knew of in the entire company. Other women were looking to me to blaze the trail, and I felt like I was letting them down.

Gamely, I kept trying. I took the loss of the promotion in stride and continued to manage my department and programs. I looked for ways to improve processes, even proposing an internal research and development study to revamp the hardware and software development process within the entire company using the total quality management principles in vogue at the time. Dick and Doug rejected the proposal. They did not implement any of the initiatives Darlene had demanded to fill the gaps in my experience. After she had lectured them about their actions during the promotion, they knew I had gone to HR and now treated me with kid gloves—but no opportunities. I knew that I had gone as far in that company as they would allow me.

The ultimate game changer

So I left—not to take care of my kids but to work for another company.

Fighting the invisible enemy

When I applied for the promotion, I went in thinking I would be judged fairly on my abilities and accomplishments. I didn't realize that my greatest perceived "weakness" was being a working mother. Dick was basing his judgment of me on his own biases and beliefs about working mothers, and how dedicated they are to their jobs. He didn't look at my own demonstrated performance: that I had come in on maternity leave to support an important test—nursing my newborn in a conference room; that I worked long hours as needed to write and submit proposals; that I consistently and successfully ran both my Engineering Department and several programs, keeping customers happy and projects on time and under budget. None of that mattered. He had decided that I couldn't be both a mother and a deputy director.

Doug clearly had the same tunnel vision. He had decided from his experience of one long-time employee's making the choice to stay home with her child that I would do the same. They didn't see *me*. They only saw the *stereotype* of me. My perceived weakness was their idea of what a working woman could and could not do. I didn't know how to fight that enemy.

Breaking the stereotype

How do you overcome someone's classification of you when it is clearly based more on a stereotype than a clear vision of your abilities? And first, how do you recognize this is what is happening?

All of us can be put into some category—or many categories—that have a stereotypical behavior. Here are a few that I have belonged to:

» Woman

» Working woman

» Mother

» Working mother

» Engineer

» West Virginia native

» Overweight

» Blonde (though currently a redhead)

» Salesperson

» Singer

Think about how someone might expect me to behave based on any one of those classifications. Perhaps you would expect me, as an engineer, to be geeky and introverted, or as a blonde, I could be ditzy. A salesperson is typically pushy and loud, right? West Virginians perhaps less educated? A mother is nurturing, but a working mother? Perhaps not so much; perhaps she is cold and indifferent—though at work she's probably not very dedicated, as she surely must prefer to be home with her children. These are not uncommon assumptions. And for me, every one of them is wrong.

Consider this: Is a father more likely to sacrifice his family time for work than a mother? That is a stereotype from the past as well. These days, not so much. Or, more accurately, *each individual is different.*

Here are a few other characteristics of me:

» Hard working

» Determined

» Competitive

» Driven and goal oriented

» Caring and compassionate

» Trustworthy

» Open minded

» Family focused

» Excellent multi-tasker

» Occasionally self-doubting

Which of these characteristics would you expect from a woman? Which from a man? How do you think a competitive, driven, hard-working woman is perceived in the workplace? Assertive, or aggressive? Strong, or bitchy? Would a man who showed his compassionate or family-focused side at work be less well respected? We need to reexamine our stereotypes.

Pay attention to how you are being perceived. You can often tell when someone is treating you according to a stereotype of some sort. If your manager expects you to clean up the conference room or take notes during a meeting, he may be (consciously or unconsciously) assigning you "female" tasks. Listen to conversations and see how men and women are referred to and if a bias is showing. Challenge that bias when you can, even—or especially—when it is not about you. "Sure, lots of men don't want to ask for directions, but Joe is always willing to reach out for assistance when he needs it."

If you feel misunderstood, preconceived notions of who you should be may be getting in the way of understanding who you really are. If that is the case, the first thing you should do is . . . continue to be yourself. The best way to break a stereotype is to not behave in a stereotypical way. Not to "act like a man" but to act like yourself, whatever that might look like. Authenticity is key and the core of how to leverage your personal power.

You may also need to call attention to your non-typical attributes to be sure they are not overlooked. I didn't broadcast my dedication to work when I brought my daughter into the office during maternity leave to support testing, but perhaps I should have. (Instead, Dick was quite uncomfortable with the notion of my nursing her in the conference room between tests.) Interestingly, nursing rooms are quite common in office environments today. I'm not sure how much this is driven by HR or if it represents a true culture shift, however.

As important as it is for your own career to battle preconceived notions of how you will behave, it also serves to crush those stereotypes for others.

Trying everything

After leaving that company, I thought long and hard about getting the Equal Employment Opportunity Commission (EEOC) involved and perhaps suing the company. They had violated laws, and I was sure I had a case, but I didn't want to be branded as a troublemaker or just another woman whining about poor treatment. In hindsight, I can't imagine that would have hurt my career, but I didn't really understand what would be involved.

More importantly, I had many friends still working there, and I didn't want to hurt them. I did look at that company as my career, and as my friends and family. I wanted it to work. I tried everything I could think of to be able to stay there while advancing my career, but in the end, I needed to go. I learned both from the fight and the loss. I learned to be stronger, not to cry in the office, to observe how women are treated early on, and decide if that is an environment I can live with. I learned that some people judge you from their own biases and not from your actual behavior. I learned to stand up for myself, even if I didn't always win.

Not all situations require such persistence. Sometimes you can easily read the writing on the wall early on and just go. But if fairness or staying at the company is important to you, you can use all the strategies at your disposal to try to achieve your goals.

CHAPTER 13

REPLACE SELF-DEFEATING THOUGHTS AND BEHAVIORS

ARE YOU YOUR OWN WORST ENEMY? What is the script running through your head as you tackle a hard problem? Do you expect to succeed or to fail?

Many women fall into the trap of believing the messages of their detractors, losing confidence in their own abilities even when they have consistently done well. Others adopt attitudes and behaviors that limit their success. To become truly successful, you need to closely examine your attitudes, behaviors, and words to see if they are helping you or hurting you.

Ways we hurt ourselves

We can't blame all our failures on other people. There may be obstacles others put in our paths, but we need to navigate around them. We cannot constantly play the victim and expect to come out on top. Learning how your own thoughts—and the behaviors they create—have an impact on your potential success is critical to changing them. What do you do to hurt yourself?

We give up too easily

Some years ago, I discovered a fantastic local *a cappella* choral group that I wanted to join. My church choir director was a member, and she encouraged me to audition. Nervous but somewhat boosted by her confidence in me, I scheduled an audition with the music director.

Filling out the information form prior to the audition, my confidence took a run for the hills. Experience? Nothing but church choir since high school. Education? Engineering doesn't count here. I had no musical training since high school chorus class. I left most of the form blank, giving it to the director with shaking hands. He looked at it quickly, then set it aside, clearly ready to get this over with. He ran me through some scales, had me sing a short tune while he tried to mess me up by playing dissonant chords beneath me, and had me sing "Amazing Grace" *a cappella*.

If you have never had to audition before, let me assure you this was a terrifying experience. Having someone judge your singing feels extremely personal. When the audition was over, the director told me briefly that there were not a lot of openings in the alto section and that I might prefer the community chorus up the road. In short, I hadn't made the cut. I left with a deflated ego, disappointed with myself and a little upset with my church choir director who had encouraged me to try.

I could have given up then, but I really wanted this. I had been to several concerts for this group, and I was in love with what they were doing and wanted to be a part of it. I joined the community chorus so I could get more experience, and the following year I signed up for another audition. Again, I didn't make it. I continued with the community chorus, and eventually signed up for private voice lessons.

I auditioned a total of five times over five years. After the fifth try, the music director stood, shook my hand, and welcomed me to the group. I had made it!

Several weeks into the season, he pulled me aside after rehearsal. "Do you know what I regret about bringing you on board?" He paused, and I felt the blood drain from my face. "That I didn't do it sooner."

I have now been with this group for over 14 years, was president of the board for three years, and even wrote and directed moving scripts for a few of our concerts. If I had given up the first time or the third or fourth time, I would still be envious of the group instead of an integral part of it.

So many times we quit at the first sign that we are not the very best at something. A critical word can kill our confidence and kick us off our paths. Don't let a detractor steal your confidence. If you falter or fail, find out what you need to improve and set goals to get back on track. If the goal is important to you, do everything you can to reach it. Take the "singing lessons"—whatever they are in your case. Take the smaller steps needed to build your strengths. You have nothing to lose and everything to gain. Wise women never give up.

We take things personally

I absolutely took it personally when I didn't succeed in my first audition. My own voice was judged and found lacking. I'm not gonna lie—that hurt. I needed a while to recover. But I had a goal, and I had strategies for improvement that would help me achieve that goal. I didn't let the setback stop me.

In business, I have also taken defeat personally, and that hurt me. When I lost the promotion to David, even knowing the playing field was tipped in his favor, I felt like a failure. I didn't want to look Dick or Doug in the eye. I tried not to mope around, but I was upset. By bringing my kids into the interview process, they had made it more personal. But for them, that was probably just a tactic to get what they wanted. For them, it was just business.

One of the hardest things to do is to *let business be business*. Not every decision will go your way, for many reasons. Few of them are personal. If you take the attitude that they are "out to get you," you lose your edge. Perhaps you don't try as hard because you know you will never win. This self-defeating thought process becomes self-ful-filling—a never-ending cycle of disappointment and affirmation of your belief that nobody likes you.

Stop it. *It's just business.* Good decisions and bad decisions are made for business reasons. The decisions are rarely personal. If you have something to work on to make yourself more valuable, do it. Otherwise, just shake off your disappointment and move on. Successful women use these small failures as opportunities for personal and professional reflection and identify the work needed to reach a desired outcome. They then adjust their game plan and try again until they succeed.

We get emotional

If it's just business, what is there to cry about? Easy for me to say, having just related a story where I cried at a most inopportune time. I have also been guilty of righteous anger in the workplace. I found an old memo I wrote (and nicely typed up, thank you very much) where I decried the fact that we were moving people around in the office too much. I was indignant and sure that my points would be taken and acted upon. Looking back, I am sure my manager had a nice little laugh and went about his business.

Being passionate about your work and caring deeply about doing the right thing are just fine, but these feelings need to be tempered with reason. Perhaps not everyone cares as much about the issues as you do or finds them minor in comparison to other problems that need solving. If you come in ranting and demanding all the time, you are not likely to get the response you are looking for.

We try to use our sexuality to move up

Being flirtatious with the boss will get you noticed—by him and by others observing your actions. It may even help you to move up, up to a point. But is that really what you want to be known for? Do you want to be "that woman," the one everyone suspects slept her way to the top? Even if you don't, but you're a big flirt, people will think that you did.

And consider this: when you are speaking to your boss or colleagues about an important matter, do you want them looking at you in a sexual way or listening to your ideas? When I was interrupted in the middle of a technical discussion by my boss' compliment on my earrings, I was thrown off my train of thought. I didn't want him to notice my earrings; I wanted him to listen to what I was saying. Imagine if I were putting off a flirtatious vibe how much he would be paying attention to my ideas.

To some extent, when men and women are working together, there may always be some sexual tension. Most of the women I interviewed were very conscious of keeping their work personas "strictly business." Becky, when she was in a sales role, frequently found herself inviting male clients to business dinners. When asked if that was ever awkward, she responded, "I was too professional in that manner, very formal. They would never second-guess where this is going. I made it very clear: we are talking shop; it's business. I don't flirt with colleagues. I put out a different vibe at work, keep it separate from private."

Becky also keeps her dress at work business-like. "I always dress the part so there is no confusion at work. Twenty years ago I was told once by a colleague, 'Keep your cleavage covered if you want to be taken seriously.' It is some of the best advice I ever got, especially working in a male-dominated field like IT where the *'marketing girl'* stereotype is still alive and well regardless of my master's degree and experience."

I am not saying you need to dress or act like a man, but you also don't want to dress to look overly sexy. Experienced women keep their work personas professional and non-flirtatious so that they can be taken seriously.

We give in too easily

It's not just giving up that can harm us. Sometimes just backing down too quickly steals our power. Many women are raised and conditioned to be nice and avoid confrontation—or they want to be helpful at all times, even to the detriment of themselves or their careers. Rather than make waves, they bring the coffee or take notes at all the meetings. Do this enough, and you may find yourself permanently in a subservient position.

Smart women learn to stand up for themselves. Practice saying no and being assertive when the situation calls for it. Professionalism always wins in the end.

Diana: Finding her strength

Even after many years of experience building her DC-area law practice—in a high-powered, highly competitive environment—Diana sometimes finds herself battling her own self-defeating thoughts. In the following story, I've italicized some of Diana's limiting thoughts and will discuss them in more detail afterward.

I was recruited to this law firm specifically to take over the practice of a partner who is retiring. Soon after I was hired, they also hired a guy (Bob) coming out of government. I found it difficult to figure out why they hired him when they had me. I have been there a year, and now the original partner is getting ready to retire. It's coming down to who is getting what. When I was hired, I was not told I'd be sharing his clients with anyone. Now this other guy is there. *I'm a team player and don't want to make waves.*

We had a meeting recently, and I found out Bob has already gotten a lot of the contacts. He has been handed the practice, because when he came in he had no existing clients. I already had a $1 million practice. I was immediately *busy doing my own thing*—helping my existing clients, not waiting for them to be handed to me. *I feel ripped off.* As we were talking about individual clients, this guy was saying 'Oh, I already have that relationship. I'll get this; I'll take that.' *It was not in my nature to say, 'That's mine.'* It's someone else's clients. They are handing it off, but *this guy was acting really aggressive*—or at least in my mind aggressive.

Diana was doing what many women do: get busy, work hard, and expect others to honor their promises. When someone else came along and started taking what was rightfully hers, she was uncomfortable standing up for herself. She viewed Bob's assertiveness—taking clients that were being turned over from the retiring partner—as aggression. Rather than being assertive herself and saying "that's mine," she watched in frustration.

Upping the ante

In addition to the individual clients Bob was grabbing from the retiring partner, another opportunity came up that could prove to be quite lucrative for the person taking over. The partner who hired Diana had a newsletter in his name that could potentially be taken over when he retired. It had been an incredibly fruitful source of business for him.

Diana proposed researching the contract to see if the newsletter could be switched to someone else or if it would be closed down when the partner retired. Bob immediately jumped in, saying he wanted to take it over. Diana said, "Wait a minute. I said let's find out the story, and you're pissing on it and saying 'It's mine.' *My natural demeanor is not to reach in and grab that*, and *I don't want to become that person*. But at the risk of losing the opportunity, it forces me into that more aggressive stance than I would ordinarily take."

Diana realized that her more passive, get-along, team-playing nature was hurting her, and she could lose a lot of business to the more assertive Bob. Responsible women take the time to understand the dynamics of the situation they are in and adjust as needed to ensure they are not left behind.

Watch your words

If you notice, Diana's own words tell us what her self-limiting thoughts are: *I'm a team player, and don't want to make waves.* There is nothing wrong with being a team player as long as everyone on the team has the same goal and is working together toward it. When one of the players starts to grab all the glory, however, it is time to look out for yourself.

I was busy doing my own thing. It is easy to get caught up in work and lose sight of the big picture. Diana had brought many clients with her and was working hard to keep them satisfied. But she also needed to pay attention to what else was happening in her firm, especially as her former partner was retiring, and his clients were coming available.

It was not in my nature to say 'That's mine.' If someone is taking something that is rightfully yours, you need to fight for it.

This guy was acting really aggressive. My natural demeanor is not to reach in and grab that, and *I don't want to become that person.* An interesting word, aggressive: ready to attack or confront, or behaving in a dominant or forceful way. Some might call his behavior "assertive": confident and direct in claiming one's rights or putting forth one's views. It sounds like Diana believes that if she were to act that way, she would be called aggressive, and she doesn't like that label. But what if she were to consider this behavior simply *assertive?* After all, she only needs to claim her rights in a confident and direct manner.

The most successful women (and men) learn to be assertive without being aggressive.

Where does it come from?

Why would a prominent lawyer with a $1 million practice be hesitant to stand up for herself? "Growing up when I did in law, women were rare. I was a junior person. This was the way you acted. You were not a ball buster as a female junior person. You needed to be smart, behind the scenes, quietly competent—not necessarily leading the charge."

Diana was used to working hard, satisfying clients, and quietly building her business. She was not conditioned to fight for herself. In spite of that, she still developed a solid reputation and respect in the law community.

> I was in a unique situation. I was married to a man I worked with many years. I was always "Mike's wife." He was a few years older, slightly ahead in law practice. You would think he was light years ahead of me. He was the guy. I was the backup person.
>
> But years later, I had a client who talked with one of our former clients. They said they hired lawyers a couple of years ago, a man and a woman, and clearly it was the woman who knew everything, and the guy was just a figurehead.

Diana's reputation continued to grow over the years, and she gained more and more satisfied clients.

Are you a success?

I was surprised when Diana told me, "I don't consider myself a success—not really." Then she explained, "It is the nature of law firms.

Every year you start at the bottom, and you all feel the need to push the rock up the hill. There is a relentless drive to bring in business."

However, Diana has been nominated as one of the top local attorneys in her field of expertise, recently listed in *Washingtonian* magazine. When pushed, she concedes:

> That's how I feel successful. Other people around the city had to vote for me. Of all the lawyers in DC, many people checked that box for me. I've worked in six law firms; I've been doing this for 31 years; I know a lot of people. A lot of people checked that box. That makes me happy. If you asked lawyers around town, I think they would say I do have knowledge of how the business works, and I'm very willing to share that. I am happy to tell people how things work. I'm generous with "Oh, here's how you might approach that."
>
> So when I get scared about the future—you never know what law firms are going to do—but there are a lot of people who would give me a reference, who would say, "She knows that cold." That makes me feel successful.

Continually building a network of other well-respected people who know and appreciate your work is a learned skill that is required to help you maintain your business credibility. Diana has done that beautifully throughout her career.

What to do about Bob?

So here is a successful, highly respected, knowledgeable lawyer who was promised the opportunity to take over a senior partner's clients when he retired. Along comes Bob who tries to take the clients away. Diana, what are you going to do about it?

"What I want to do is quit—say 'Fuck you' and take my business and go. But when I think about it, no, hell no—I want to fight. I have not tapped into my strength, and I need to. I have called some of the clients and discovered that I know most of them already."

Diana should be able to approach this from a position of power. To be able to say to the partners, "Here is what I was promised, and here is what is happening. I still want to take over the business. What's going on here?"

Diana is fortunate to be working with a career coach provided to partners at her firm. Diana's coach frequently asks her, "What do you need? And why are you not asking for that?" That is a very good mantra for all of us: *What do you need? And why are you not asking for that?*

Too little, too late. Where have we heard that before?

Diana did fight back and did take over some of the retiring partner's clients. But she also realized this law firm didn't have her back and wasn't a great fit for her needs:

> Ultimately, the conflict that was created by hiring some new lawyers forced me to choose to fire one of my clients or leave; so I left and took the client with me. They tried to keep some of them, but the ones whom I had personal relationships with all chuckled and said, "No, thank you." I brought some with me (mostly ones I had generated) and didn't

bring others. I felt good about it. I am much more appreciated here.

Diana tapped into her strength and fought for what was hers. Her decision to leave made sense, as she was able to retain key clients rather than release them due to conflicts with lawyers hired after her. She knew that no one was going to look after her career for her, so she took it into her own hands to manage. This is a powerful stance by a successful woman.

Finding your own strength

You know when your strength is slipping, when you are feeling like you are no longer in control of your career. You find yourself saying "Yes" when in your heart, you want to fight. You start to take things personally or get emotional over business decisions. You lose your confidence, give in too easily. You don't want to make waves or be seen as bitchy or aggressive.

All these are self-defeating thoughts and behaviors. They are not helping you in any way. If you catch yourself doing it, stop and reassess. Tap into your personal power. Fight the urge to give up.

If you can turn around these limiting beliefs, your career can take off. Ask yourself: *What do I need? Why am I not asking for it?* Then ask for it. No, demand it. You are worth it.

CHAPTER 14

FINDING
THE POSITIVE

WHEN ENCOUNTERING OBSTACLES in the work-
place, you may see only the negative. If you are not careful, you can
sink into negative attitudes when things are not going your way.
Unfortunately, this can result in your being branded as a complainer,
which is a very hard downward spiral to break out of.

Women who look for the positive in situations and strive to
surround themselves with other positive people are the ones who
succeed.

A learned behavior

I have been guilty of sinking into negative attitudes myself and have
found it to really hurt me in the long run. In my early career, I paid
attention to what was working and where the problems were, and I
tried to effect change—sometimes with a little too much righteous
indignation.

As I mentioned in the last chapter, I recently found a three-page typed memo I sent to the vice president of my company regarding office space. Three pages. I thoroughly examined all the possible options for placement of three new employees and took issue with their placing the new employees on a separate floor from their colleagues. I cringed when I read, "We can continue to solve the short-term problems in our tradition of short-term solutions, or we can attempt some long-range planning." What did I hope to accomplish with this insult? Holy smokes, I was naive!

When I brought issues up to management, I was usually passionate and forceful in my argument. I was told on more than one occasion to "Calm down," which really set my blood to boiling. But I learned that they didn't respond well to angry suggestions, and I started to tone down my arguments and present well-thought-out solutions. These were much better received, even if they were not implemented.

If you find yourself upset about something at work that you think needs changing, take a step back. Rather than storm in with a complaint, you really want to formulate a suggestion or solution to bring to the conversation. Management is much more receptive to suggestions than complaints. And please, no veiled insults at their inability to make a proper decision.

Watch the whining

After I was passed over for the promotion, I started really looking around at things. Not only had I apparently hit the very low glass ceiling but the women in Publications were also treated like a commodity. The one woman in management besides me was considered by many as just running a "body shop," with no real technical or management skills (I'm sure an unfair assessment). Even my well-thought-out suggestions for improvements were dismissed with barely a comment. Opportunities for women to move up were non-existent. When the mandates by HR to give me the experience management had said I lacked were not implemented, I decided I needed to go.

When I changed companies, I moved from a fast-paced management and system engineering position to a role as an engineer writing test plans—something I could practically do in my sleep. At first, being part of a small company launching a new business was exciting, but there were a lot of problems. I was bored with my actual job and unhappy about some of the decisions management was making. So were a lot of others in the company. I found myself at the center of a lot of whining among my colleagues. Everyone flocked to me and unloaded their complaints on me, and I supported them in their negativity.

This was not good, and I knew it. Everyone wanted me to bring the complaints to management, for some reason believing that I could effect change. I decided to pull together all the issues into a single document, even calling a secret meeting to make sure I captured everything. I knew I would have one shot at presenting this to management.

Pushing for improvement

I made an appointment with the VP of engineering and came in with the two-page list of issues. I started by saying there was a morale problem in the company, and the VP immediately sprang to the defensive. "If there were I morale problem, I would know it!" he insisted.

"For some reason, people are comfortable talking with me," I responded, trying to bring him back in. "They may feel awkward bringing their issues to you, and they have asked me to present them. I hope you don't mind."

From his facial redness, tight lips, and crossed arms, I concluded he clearly did mind. I pushed ahead anyway—went through the list in detail, until we got about halfway through it. He snatched it from me, slammed it down on his desk, and said, "I don't believe people have these issues. You are making this shit up. I'll get to the bottom of this; don't you worry." With that, he turned his back to me, and I was dismissed—and stunned.

He called an all-hands meeting the next day, brandishing the list in front of a room full of sheepish employees. "Who knew about this?" he asked. Most of the room raised their hands but didn't meet his eyes. He started going through the list, asking them to corroborate what I had reported. When he could see that I hadn't made it up, he threw the list down on the table.

"Fine. You all have complaints. Now you sit in this room together until you have documented everything you want fixed with the proposed solutions. Matt, I want you to bring it to me afterward, and we will see what we can do." He stormed out of the room, not looking at me.

I was the messenger of bad news for a group of people, and I was going to suffer for it. At the time, though, I was stunned. I felt quite righteous bringing the issues to the forefront. We worked on the list and made suggestions, and Matt got to bring them to the VP. No changes were made.

In hindsight, I think it was a mistake for me to wallow in negativity and listen to everyone's complaints. We supported each other in our misery rather than look for the positive in our situation or even try to make small changes to improve it. I've heard this referred to as creating negative agreement. Getting caught up in the whining is all too easy but gets you nowhere. Productivity suffers when you are unhappy, even beyond the time wasted sitting around complaining.

Misery may love company, but companies don't like misery. Snap out of it. Clever women focus on how to create positive change where they can, or walk away when they can't.

Negativity toward you

When I left that company for another opportunity, I also made a career change to applications engineering and ultimately sales and marketing director for a new hardware line developed by the company. As I mentioned in Chapters Two and Four, I found myself the lone female manager in a small company with male bosses, male and female engineers, and female support staff. In my role, I gave frequent taskings to the support staff, as they helped with processing orders and leads and ordering marketing materials, etc. I was kind and polite in asking for things and thankful when tasks were complete.

Still, the women hated me. It took me a while to figure that out, as I often got the passive-aggressive response, "Sure, I'll do it" with no intention of following through. They barely spoke to me outside of the needs of the job and stopped any conversation they were having when I entered the room.

I had no idea why they disliked me or what to do about it. They seemed to have no issues with the women engineers, but they weren't being directly tasked by them. They had no issues doing things for my boss, a man. And they got along well with the CEO's wife, who ran the Accounting Department. In fact, she took to insulting me in meetings both in front of me and when I wasn't present.

This was my first experience with negativity directed toward me—at least from women. When I told my former colleagues at previous jobs, they were shocked. "How could they not like you?" I tried to mend things—not even sure what I had broken. I was exceedingly polite, complimentary, and thankful for anything they did for me. Nothing worked.

So I decided it was business, and they needed to do their jobs whether they liked me or not. I tried not to take it personally (though it still hurt) and proceeded as if their dislike didn't exist. If they pulled the passive-aggressive shit, I called them out on it, in front of my boss: "Oh, I thought you were going to take care of that. What happened?" In spite of them, I successfully grew sales beyond any expectations. I hired a marketing manager and applications engineers to work for me and moved into a director role.

As much as we all want to be liked, that's not always possible. As a friend of mine likes to say, "I'm not everyone's cup of gin." Enduring negativity focused at you is difficult, but it can't always be avoided.

Business is business

When Anne started out as a paralegal, she had a female secretary who was a little bit older than she was:

> She did not like doing my work at all. I have found that sometimes people have resentments, whatever they are—racism, sexism, ageism, etc. I've gotta tell you: I don't care. Business is business. I've made it very clear, "You do not have to like me. I don't even care; we don't hang out. But business is business, and you don't ever make the mistakes that you did."

And she did it purposefully. When my supervisor told her she had to continue to do my work, she quit. Was it because I was a woman? Was it because I was a black woman? Was it because I was younger? Was it because I was educated and she felt some resentment? I don't know, but I didn't care. I still don't care. Business is business, and we have to do business. Now if we're gonna be friends, this is an easy decision. We're not gonna be friends.

When attitudes toward you are negative, you can try to figure out why, and make changes if they are possible. But if you are treating people with respect and they just don't like you, there is not much to be done. Remember that business is business. It's not a popularity contest.

The Pollyanna manager

In one company I worked for, there were many problems delivering the products and services I had sold, and the customer was unhappy. My job as an account manager included bringing the customer's concerns to management to see what could be done about them. Unfortunately, my manager didn't want to hear anything negative, and he constantly tried to turn things around as being not so bad—not to solve them, necessarily, but to convince me that everything was fine.

"Yes, it's true we won't be able to deliver the T-1 lines for six more months, even though we promise two months in the contract. I'm sure the customer will understand. They are lucky to have us at such a great price."

I wanted nothing more than to hear him say, just once, "That sucks." He could have then gone on to tell me how to solve it, and I would have been thrilled. Instead, because of his steadfast refusal to believe anything negative was happening, I became more and more strident about the issues I was confronting every day. I found others who were also unhappy about things, and we complained together both about the problems and about Mike's refusal to acknowledge them. I didn't feel heard, so I just got louder.

In the end, the customer became so unhappy they asked for me to be removed from the account—blaming me for the inability of the company to deliver on what they had promised. I was thrown under the bus. The company moved me onto a different part of the account rather than fight for me with the customer. I had warned them about everything.

I'm not sure what I could have done differently in that situation, though I certainly don't think my relentless complaining about the issues was a great solution. I probably could have worked harder to formulate ideas for improvement and present them with a positive spin for my Pollyanna boss. Or if he was a roadblock to change, I could have found a way around him. After all, the issues were impacting my company's reputation with this important customer.

A larger lesson may be for those in management positions whose employees bring complaints or problems to you: Make sure the employees feel *heard*. If something sucks, say it; then get on with trying to fix it. Even if it sucks, and you know you can't fix it, don't insult the employee by pretending everything is okay. I would have been just fine with hearing, "This is not ideal, but here is why we can't change it right now. What can we do to work around it?" Perceptive women know that **how** you deliver information is key. Acknowledging the problem, even if there is no immediate fix, buys you credibility with others and keeps your integrity intact.

The perils of being remote

In my first job as a remote, home-based employee, I "attended" most meetings by phone. I was the first remote employee in the company, and therefore they were not used to having someone on the other end of the phone line. Sometimes they would forget to dial me in, and I would be frantically trying to figure out what conference room they were in and what the phone number was for the room. As a result, I often "arrived" late for a meeting, slightly annoyed that they had forgotten me and interrupting their meeting in progress. I usually didn't know who else was in the room on the other end, what they were saying, or how they were interpreting what I said. If I sounded annoyed at being forgotten, that's all they heard. Most of them had never even met me, as I was hundreds of miles from the home office and didn't get up there more than a couple times a year. They had no positive framework for me, just a voice on the other end of the line sometimes trying to get a word in when they were having a heated discussion around the table.

"Excuse me. Hello! Hello? Can I say something?" If someone was talking in the room, they didn't even hear me on the conference phone, because it was single duplex: one direction at a time. By the time I got their attention, I was often seriously irritated, or the moment for my comment had passed. I don't know what kind of looks were passed around in the conference room when my voice came through, but I suspect they weren't smiles and happy nods. I became branded as being negative.

When I complained to my boss about the problems with the remote meetings, he told me I needed to stop complaining. When

I expressed frustration with my extremely slow computer connection and a technical support staff unused to working with a remote employee, he put in my performance review that I had a negative attitude. I gave up on effecting change by bringing up issues and tried to project a more positive attitude. After all, I hated seeing that on my performance evaluations, and my goal was to keep the job.

My change of attitude came too late. I couldn't shake the negative attitudes toward me or about me. When I asked for a quick turnaround on getting an engineer assigned to support me with a customer meeting, I was told in my performance review that I had "no respect for anyone else's time."

This is a real danger for remote employees, especially if you rarely meet your colleagues face to face. If your only contact is a disembodied voice on the phone, your tone of voice projects much more than you might intend. You also lose the contextual clues of body language and facial expression in response to what you are saying, so you might not notice when you are not being well received. In a face-to-face conversation, you can take that in and adjust what you are saying, either consciously or unconsciously.

Because of this, projecting a positive attitude is even more important as a remote employee. Stand and smile when you are talking; this will come through in your voice. Ask in advance for whoever is running the meeting to tell you who is in the room and to give you a chance to speak along with others. If you can use a video conference, even if that means you have to change out of your pajamas for the meeting, you will get to see who is talking in the room, and they will get to know you better by seeing you.

As a remote employee, if you can spend some time in the office on a somewhat regular cadence (i.e., monthly, quarterly, etc.), then you can build relationships with colleagues and be seen as more than just a name on an org chart or a voice on a phone call. That wasn't an option for me, unfortunately. Instead, I probably should have reached out to colleagues more regularly, asking their advice or sharing interesting information about the industry—anything to build a more positive relationship. Turning around someone's negative impression of you is much harder than maintaining a positive attitude.

Negative company culture

The attitude of a company toward its employees can make a huge difference in their satisfaction with work. Unfortunately, at this company where I was remote, there was a very negative company culture. As I mentioned in Chapter Three, the performance evaluation forms were even structured that way: five bullet points for your strengths and five pages for your areas for improvement. They looked at it as an environment for "continuous improvement." In reality, this approach put pressure on managers to catch you doing something wrong so they would have something to write about on your performance evaluation. At least, that's how things turned out for me.

Once my manager decided I was negative, he interpreted everything I did under that microscope. If I sent him a private email asking for changes to improve my experience with remote conference meetings, he put that in my review as being a complainer. Others who complained about issues at the company were impolitely shown the door. Clearly, only those who "drank the Kool-Aid" and said nothing but nice things about the company were going to stick around. My goal was to keep the job, so I shut my mouth.

If you find yourself in a company with a negative attitude toward its employees, think carefully about whether that is a place you can thrive. If you can put your head down, think only about the positive things, and ignore the attitude, perhaps you can. But if you find the atmosphere stifles your creativity or kills your motivation, get out early. Continuing to work in that kind of environment is very difficult. Before you know it, you may sink to their level, especially if you are promoted and expected to look for the negative in others around you.

Finally, a positive experience

The first few weeks at my current company, I was worried. I spoke to the other salespeople in the company and was regaled with tales of all that was wrong:

» "Marketing doesn't get it. They are clueless about our products, and nothing they produce is helpful."

» "There are no leads coming in."

» "The market is tapped out."

Then I went on a three-day road trip with three colleagues—a business development person, an inside sales guy, and an engineer. They spent the three days in the car whining and complaining about all the problems with the company, the customers, the products, and management. "Just trying to warn you. You need to know these things." "You are the golden child now and have the ear of management. You can get them to listen and fix everything."

What had I gotten myself into? I had no intention of bringing all their complaints to management—that had backfired on me once before, and besides, they weren't really issues I was that concerned about. I had interviewed carefully with all the top management at the company, including the CEO, and I believed in what they were doing.

Rather than being sucked into the negative morass, I decided to take a more positive approach. I found others in the company who were happy with their jobs, talked with them about the good things, and gained some insight into the source of the negativity in others. Instead of creating negative agreement, I worked on creating an atmosphere of positive agreement. I listened to the complaints of those who were unhappy and filtered them through my own experience. It really wasn't that bad.

Every company has its "stuff." No place is perfect. If you are expecting perfection, you will be sorely disappointed in your life. If you look only for the negative, you will find it. If, instead, you look for the positive, you will undoubtedly find some of that as well. See if it is enough to build on.

In my case, I took the helpful ideas from my colleagues, set aside the negativity, and just started doing my job. In meetings, I talked about the good things happening and suggested ways we could do even more good things. I achieved early and sustained success, rising to the top of the sales charts quickly and staying there. Ultimately, my contributions were further recognized, and I was able to move up, form a team, and become a key part of the sales management organization. Accomplished women find positive, like-minded people to work with that want to help drive business success.

Meanwhile, those with negative attitudes were slowly being weaned from the company, either through attrition or deliberately. My company wanted to foster a supportive, positive environment. I wasn't the only one who had noticed the complainers.

I fully believe that my decision to focus on the positive is responsible for my success at this company. I work harder than ever, because I am happy. I love my customers, my colleagues, and my products.

I also believe that the company's culture of support and positivity will reap benefits for years to come. Management is thrilled to adopt my suggestions, because I present them in a positive way and show results. We are hiring others with a similar positive attitude, and we support and nurture that culture. Happy people do good work.

Changing yourself

Switching your attitude from negative to positive can require real effort. You can feel hopeless when you see so many problems. If the people around you are complaining all the time, you may easily fall in alongside them. Misery loves company.

Take stock periodically. See if you are falling into the trap of negativity. If you are, see if you can find something positive to focus on. Talk to people who are more upbeat and build on their energy. If the people around you are whining and complaining all the time, take a step away. You can even try to influence their attitudes by pointing out something good, but don't expect everyone to want to change. The only one you can really change is yourself.

To have a positive attitude is not to be a Pollyanna, ignoring problems and pretending everything is wonderful. Instead, a positive attitude develops resilience, durability, buoyancy, and the determination to keep going. The benefits are immeasurable. With a positive outlook, you can achieve so much more.

CHAPTER 15

DEFINING
YOUR OWN SUCCESS

SMART WOMEN are often driven and feel a need to move up at all costs. If they don't succeed in reaching the top, they can feel like they have failed to live up to their own expectations or those of others.

What makes you feel successful? Do you need to reach the very top of your career ladder, or can you achieve success along the way? What if you decide to change paths—does this somehow make you a failure on your original path? Of course not. If you don't feel this way and you just want to work hard at your current level, that's ok too. Empowered women bring their best no matter where they are!

Single-focused or broad-focused success?

Some people have a very clear focus on what their goals are and exactly where they need to be to feel they have achieved their goals. This can be a certain job title or level at their current job, such as becoming a partner in their law firm. Or it can be a goal of forming their own company or moving up to director or vice president or CEO of an existing company.

If you have a specific plan for your career and will measure your degree of success by how well you are following your plan, you are single-focused. This is not a bad thing. With that in mind, however, you will need to consider whether sacrifices may need to be made in other areas of your life to achieve these goals. Realistically evaluating the effort needed will help you plan your life around the career goal. You may decide to defer having children, for example, or make sure you have a good childcare arrangement and/or supportive partner.

Others are less driven toward a single measurement of success, or life circumstances or opportunities cause them to redirect their focus. Many people consider it more important to find a balance in their lives between work and family or other interests. They may consider themselves a success if they are able to have a challenging and rewarding career while maintaining a happy home life or a fun avocation—such as jazz singing, swing dancing, or writing (a few of my outside interests).

Whether your goals are single-focused or broad, they are your own. You define your goals, and you define how and when you achieve them. Nobody else can tell you if you are a success—that is entirely up to you. At the end of the day, you are the boss of you. Don't expect others to have the same focus that you do on your goals.

How do you even measure this?

Diana, the highly regarded attorney in Chapter 13, had to be talked into believing she was a success. She is a partner in her firm, bringing in over $1 million worth of client business each year. She was nominated by her peers as one of the top attorneys in her area of expertise. She has an extensive network of clients and colleagues who think very highly of her. Yet her initial answer to the question, "Are you successful?" was "Not really."

Maybe she was just being modest. After some discussion she was able to admit that yes, she considers herself successful.

Why are we so hard on ourselves? Would Diana have needed to be the #1 attorney in the United States—how would you even measure that? Are you not a success until you are managing partner in a large law firm? How large does it have to be?

There is no objective measure of success. You don't have to be CEO of a major firm to be successful. You don't have to be at the top of any particular ladder. You don't have to push, fight, and claw to a specific position just so you can say you are a success.

Success is simply the attainment of a goal. You get to define your own goals and celebrate your achievements. A clever woman defines her own success on her own terms and drives toward her goals with determination.

Keep your head in your own game

Ah, jealousy, that green-eyed monster. How tempting it is to look at our neighbor, coworker, or high school friend on Facebook and think, *They are successful. Why can't I have that?*

Rarely do we see the ugly side of someone else's achievements. We don't always see the sacrifices they make, the opportunities they have passed up to get where they are, or the mistakes they made along the way and learned to recover from. Not many people post on Facebook that they screwed up the Robinson account and are now groveling to keep their job.

And we rarely see the good side, either: how hard they worked, how much they studied the competition or the customer to know exactly what to say to win the business. Or how their basic kindness and helpfulness and teamwork won them the respect of colleagues and managers who then helped them to move up.

I could tell you not to pay attention to what others are doing, but that's a little short-sighted. You can learn from the successes and failures of your coworkers. The more you see and understand how they are achieving their goals, the more you can emulate them. The more you watch someone recover from a failure, the more empathic you might be, and the better you might recover from your own mistakes.

Beyond these lessons, forget what anyone else around you is achieving. Don't compare yourself to others if that is going to make you jealous. Keep your head in your own game. Life isn't always fair, so whining about how someone else is getting "special treatment" is not helping anyone. Do your job; improve yourself; define and work toward your own success.

Blazing the trail

Sheila started her marketing career in the late seventies working for a large automotive company. She was promoted to a job that had never been held by a woman before. An older woman in her department made a big deal of it. "They're going to be watching you to see who you eat lunch with—the women or the men." So she mixed it up–ate with both. Later, when they transferred her to New Jersey, she found out they had never transferred a woman before. The older woman again told her, "What you decide will impact the women that come along behind you." Sheila felt the pressure of breaking a glass ceiling she had not been aware of.

"I got to Newark, and there was one other woman doing the same thing I was doing. I always felt like I had to prove myself. I wanted to feel like I was capable and I could do it." She also felt she needed to set a good example for women so that others following her could also be given opportunities.

"I felt respected there. But when they decided to close the New Jersey office, they were going to move us all back to Michigan. My boss' boss was going around with the clipboard asking if people were going to go—yes or no. He came to my desk and said, 'Yes, right?' and I said, 'Nope.' Blew his mind. I felt valued and have always felt valued. I've been pretty lucky." Even as Sheila left the company for a new opportunity, she knew that she had done well both for herself and for women coming along behind her. She was successful in achieving her goals at that company.

Some might say that the glass ceiling no longer exists—that enough women have been in positions of power that there are no obstacles anymore. Untrue. Women are still blazing trails in new companies, industries, and positions all the time. Many industries continue to be male-dominated, and women need to work as hard as ever to achieve their goals in these areas.

If you find yourself in or striving for a "first"—first woman director in your company, for example—remember that you are fighting not just for yourself but for future generations of women. Your success can be that much sweeter to know you are helping others along the way.

Having your success stolen

Sheila took her experience with the automotive group to her new position as senior marketing director at a startup satellite company. She successfully developed and implemented new marketing strategies, coordinated advertising and public relations, worked with Engineering to refine product offerings, and led the startup of customer service, training, user groups, etc. She loved working for a startup, where her skills could be used in multiple ways, and everyone made a difference in the success of the company.

Unfortunately, the market could not sustain the costs of operating the satellites, and the company was forced to declare bankruptcy. Sheila had to move on. Happily, she brought her skills and experience with her and recognized a huge opportunity for her new company to capture revenue from customers for software updates that were previously provided for free:

> I did all the work to create this program from scratch. What they were doing was the engineers would send out software fixes and would include new features, but they weren't getting any revenue for the new features. They couldn't keep track of what software customers had, so it was a nightmare trying to maintain the systems. So I came in and productized the software, which included getting it manufactured in their plant. No more from the engineers to the customers; it had to go through our customer service group. I implemented auditing procedures, so you could audit the customer systems and bring them up to the current level across their platforms. I put together pricing and materials to educate the sales force on how to sell it. It was quite a project. I had never done anything like that before, so it was kind of, "Jump right in and do it."
>
> But the first year it went great: over $1M sales for the program. I was not on commission for the

sales, just a flat salary. Then they gave it to my boss to run. They decided a woman can't run this—it's getting too big—even though she's the one that created it."

Sheila's success was once again stolen from her, this time because she was a woman. She had to weigh whether to fight or move on. "I actually went to a lawyer or agency for discrimination. They said I had a really good case, but to go through all that? It's not worth it. You don't have any quick recourse when that stuff happens. You just leave, which is what I ended up doing." As painful as it was to create this complex and profitable program, then have it taken from her, Sheila felt successful. She took pride in her accomplishments and took with her the valuable experience of the situation that she could use elsewhere.

We can't always dictate what happens with our work product. Sometimes companies need to make decisions that eliminate our projects, hand them off to others to run, or even lay us off. That does not mean we did not succeed in what we were doing. Successful women learn to celebrate accomplishments along the way, and then bring the skills and experience gained to the next set of goals.

How high is high enough?

Sheila moved on, continuing to bring her expertise and experience to new companies and new projects. She has been a sales director, program director, senior capture manager, and director of capture management. (Capture managers work on long-term business development opportunities for large companies.) She has earned the respect of her peers, customers, and management. She enjoys her job, rising to new challenges continuously. She has been a manager but prefers her work as an individual contributor. She is involved in industry associations and has a rich network of contacts. She was a pioneer for women in her industry and has mentored others. Though she is not a VP or CEO, Sheila is clearly a success.

"I never had aspirations to be a VP. You're on this pedestal, and you get knocked down so easily, caught up in politics. I like the work that I'm doing. I've always been happy being at the level I'm at—keep my nose down and working and out of the political stuff. Individual contributor. I love this." Each of us needs to set our own goals and aspirations for what level we want to achieve in our careers. Some will want to be CEO, and others are content at lower levels than that.

Changing your definition

When I first started out as a young engineer, my ambitions were very high. I moved up quickly and had every intention of continuing to climb the ladder—straight to the top. I had no problem envisioning myself as a vice president, president, or even CEO of a company.

My first setback was losing the promotion to deputy director, with the resulting change of company and responsibilities. I realized that the first company was not going to allow me to achieve my goals, so I made a lateral move—even a step back in my career—from manager of 20 engineers to individual contributor. Reality started to settle in, both with the obstacles in my career and later in my personal life, as I got divorced and became a single parent of two small children. I had a family and didn't want to work 80-hour weeks to reach the top.

I readjusted my vision. When I moved from engineering to high-tech sales, I changed my career path and increased my income. I found success in creating and managing the Sales and

Marketing Department at a small company, then found my growth path there to be limited by the risk aversion of the "mom and pop" owners.

I tried a different path. I tripled sales again at a new company but left when they couldn't deliver on promises and put my reputation at risk.

Over time, my goals changed. My life was more than just work. I didn't want the pressure and intense time commitment of trying to move up the corporate ladder, and frankly, I hadn't yet been a part of a corporation I really wanted to run.

I have been in jobs where I felt successful and some where I didn't. For too long in the job before this one, my mantra was "the goal is to keep the job." Not because it was so awesome, but because I had the flexibility to work from home, and it paid well. Thankfully, I am now with a company I love, am extremely successful in my job, and see a future where I continue to grow and move up as the company grows. My children are now grown, and I use my time outside work to pursue my many passions: singing, dancing, writing, playing bridge.

There is nothing wrong with adjusting your vision as you gain experience and knowledge. You can't expect to know your end game when you are just starting out. Strong women know that work-life balance is key and that change offers the opportunity to reinvent yourself.

What else constitutes success?

Success can be simply defined as a favorable or desired outcome, or the accomplishment of one's goals. Too many people narrow that definition to equate to the attainment of wealth, a title, respect, or fame, but there can be many different desired outcomes in life.

Many people want to make a difference in the world—whether through social programs, teaching, or even developing products that make life easier. Others want to provide a comfortable living for their families. Some want to use their talents and creativity and share them with the world. Others want to feel the satisfaction of a job well done, regardless of what the job is.

Take a careful look at your goals in life, not just your career aspirations. Make sure all is in alignment and achievable, and make adjustments over time. If you aspire to run your own company but are a single parent of four young children, you are going to need help. Remember, a savvy woman defines success on her own terms and drives toward her goals with determination.

CHAPTER 16

RECOVERING FROM DEFEAT

YOU'RE SMART, AMBITIOUS, and hard-working. Likely you got good grades in school and are doing well and moving up in your organization. You are used to succeeding. What do you do the first time (or any time) you fail at something? Can you accept that things don't always go well for you? Can you pick yourself up and move on? And can you learn from your mistakes—or from the mistreatment you've received at the hands of other people?

It's not my fault

Often our first instinct is to blame others when things go wrong. Sometimes, the failure really is not our fault, even if we suffer from it. Savvy women examine closely our part in the situation to see if there are things we can learn from it. Perhaps we could have done better.

I was working for a very small company in 2000–2001, selling software to engineers. When I joined the company, my manager bragged about how much money he was making, implying that I would certainly enjoy the same level of success. I was relatively new to sales and only realized later that he had cherry-picked all the best-performing accounts for himself, leaving me to dig up all new customers in the territory. The industry was in a decline at that time, and the software was very complex—all making it very difficult to find and nurture new customers. I was not the only one in the company struggling, and by August 2001 the company stock was delisted, and half the employees were laid off—including me.

Not my fault, right? My manager took all the good accounts. The software was hard to sell. The market was declining. Other salespeople were also having trouble selling. All true. But not the whole story.

I had some success with the software, made a pretty major deal with a large company. I had done extremely well in the two sales positions I held previously, but this was completely different. I had little experience with prospecting, cold-calling, and bringing in net new business. I hadn't been formally trained or coached in sales, aside from a few short courses. I didn't know what to do—and I was afraid to admit it. I spent hours in my office searching the web for companies to contact but not enough hours actually making calls or getting out to see people. I kept my big customer happy—that I was good at—and tried to expand out within that company to no avail.

I hated the feeling I wasn't doing my job well, but I didn't ask for help. I was filled with self-doubt. Even though I saw the company going downhill, I didn't fear for my job, because I had made the one big sale that was continuing to bring in business. I was laid off in August 2001. That was partly my own fault.

As much as we may not want to admit we don't know everything, doing so is critical to our continued growth and success. Don't let pride keep you from asking for help. If you do, you have only yourself to blame if you don't succeed in a task or job. Responsible women know when to ask for help and see getting help as an opportunity to learn something—not as a failure.

Holy shit! Now what?

Days after my layoff, I went on a previously planned trip to New York City. On August 11, 2001, I had lunch with my mom and a friend at Windows of the World at the top of the World Trade Center. I imagine the lovely staff that waited on us that day lost their lives a month later, on 9/11. Sort of puts my problem in perspective.

But I was a single mother of two with no job. After my two weeks of severance, I qualified for unemployment, which barely paid for COBRA health insurance for the kids and me. That left mortgage, utilities, food, insurance, gas, etc. on no income. Thankfully, I had some savings, but this period was going to be rough. Finding a new job was going to be difficult. The industry was in decline even before 9/11, and nothing much was happening for months after, as the country and the world attempted to recover.

On a more personal level, my self-esteem took a nosedive. My family was counting on me, and I had let them down. I had never been fired before—okay, laid off, but it felt the same. I knew I hadn't been doing my best, which made it worse. My confidence was shot. I would look in the paper and online at job listings and think to myself, *I could never do that*. I didn't even want to apply, because surely they would see what a failure I was.

I managed to snag one interview, and the manager grilled me on individual deals that I couldn't remember the details of. He told me he didn't believe I had sold anything. I didn't get the job and decided I was lucky to not be working for such a jerk.

Eventually, I got into the swing of things. I set up my computer in my home office and spent time each day researching and applying for jobs. It took six months. In January 2002, I started working from home, selling software to engineers.

Lessons learned

The most powerful women can keep things in perspective, stay grounded, and realize that challenges are teachable moments to help drive growth. I make it a habit to look for the positive in any situation or at least a lesson learned from the experience. I was grateful that I wasn't working and traveling on 9/11. I needed to be with my family as we all processed what had happened and what might still happen. I was not stranded somewhere else when the planes stopped flying over the United States for weeks.

I learned, by working from home each day looking for a job, that I could consider a home-based sales position, which are common in my industry. I had always thought I could never be motivated enough to do that. I have now been doing it for 17 years. I loved being here when my children came home from school to tell me about their days.

I learned that I was not indispensable. That was a hard lesson. Even though I outperformed some of the other salespeople in my company, I was let go. From that I knew that I needed to ask for help when needed and have a financial safety net in case it happened again. It did.

Second verse: Same as the first, a whole lot louder and a whole lot worse

I lasted twelve years at that company. The first few years were excellent though certainly not perfect. I was selling something I believed in that was well accepted in my industry. I loved working from home, though I was frustrated by those at headquarters who forgot to dial me in for meetings and such. I was successful. I sold one of the first of my company's enterprise licenses—a long, complex, and difficult sale that brought in millions of dollars for my company (not for me). I exceeded my quota each year and received performance awards many times.

I had learned a valuable lesson. When things were a problem, or I needed something, I asked for help. As I mentioned in an earlier chapter, that got me branded as a complainer.

I learned a new lesson: don't make waves about lesser things when a more important goal is at stake personally or professionally. The goal was to keep the job—not a lofty goal, to be sure, but I mostly liked what I was doing, the flexibility of working from home, and the income.

But the negative corporate culture I described in Chapter 14 was wearing me down. I felt drained. I didn't fit with the sports-loving, back-slapping sales guys and managers at corporate headquarters. As a remote employee, I had very little connection to my colleagues. I would go to the company kickoff and feel alone among thousands of people.

In spite of my successful track record of sales, they took away the major accounts I had worked for nine years and gave me a geographic territory, where I would need to do more prospecting and lots of smaller sales. This geographic territory was loaded with small contractors feeling the blow of government sequestration—which

YOU HAVE WHAT IT TAKES

meant they were buying nothing. They took away my sales support network. They fired my manager and put me in a group with people who still had major accounts. They did nothing to help me learn to work the geographic territory. This time, I asked for help but got little. I think they were hoping I would quit. I wish I had.

Instead, they upped their game against me—went with me to customer meetings, found things to criticize, and saved up the criticisms for performance reviews rather than taking corrective action when it could make a difference. The new VP of sales set unreasonably high expectations for numbers of customer meetings and other key performance indicators (KPIs). They reorganized the sales force and took away my inside sales support person. I felt like I could not win, and that destroyed my motivation and my spirit.

The final blow

In spite of everything, I kept on plugging. My first clue things were going downhill fast was when nobody in sales management could look me in the eye during the sales kickoff (SKO). After 12 years, they treated me as if I didn't exist.

When my manager made arrangements to fly into town to deliver my performance review, I knew something was up. That was usually something we took care of during SKO. I met my manager in a conference room at the hotel airport, and he immediately called his boss to join in the meeting by phone. This was not normal. Butterflies in my stomach, I sat down and received the paper handed to me. It was not a performance review but a performance improvement plan—a PIP—an unreasonable set of goals I needed to achieve in the next five weeks, or I would be let go.

I was stunned. I had ended the prior year at 95% of quota in a challenging territory due to government shutdown and sequestration. Of the 72 sales reps in the company, only 14 exceeded quota. I was in the top 1/3 in quota performance. I was in the top 16 reps in the other KPIs.

Just by being put on the PIP, I was made ineligible for bonuses for my performance from the past year. This wasn't business. It was personal.

The expectations in the PIP were ludicrous. I needed to track and report on my activities for every hour of every day in a weekly detailed report. I was to research and bring information on 75 new companies in my territory that had never purchased from us before. I was to do five customer visits per week. I was to add 150 new names to the contact list through prospecting activities. The deadline on all of it was in less than five weeks. I had no inside salesperson at this point, so I was also doing all the lead follow up, order processing, and chasing down $30 tax issues on an average of 60 orders per month.

They had set me up to fail. The goal of a PIP is to break you down and make you leave. They didn't expect me to hit the numbers.

I worked a ridiculous number of hours per week and did it anyway. I hit those damn numbers. I spent the rest of my hours not sleeping but looking for a new job.

After five weeks, I turned in my data, and they carefully combed through it. They found one of my 75 identified new accounts had spent $300 with us two years ago. They told me that in addition to what they had explicitly spelled out for my expectations, I should also have converted the new accounts into active opportunities. They decided I failed.

This time my manager didn't fly into town. I got on a conference call with him and his boss late on a Friday afternoon. They sent me another PIP—this time with a two-week deadline and more unachievable numbers. When I indicated I thought the goals were unachievable, I was told, "If you sign this, you are saying that you think it is doable." It was not.

"What are my options?" I asked. I heard my boss' boss whispering in the background, "Tell her to call HR." "You can call Human Resources to see what your options are."

This was all they hoped it would be. HR informed me I could take an exit package: 12 weeks of 60% pay for my 12 years of service, no commissions effective immediately, immediate cancellation of my health insurance and all other benefits, no unemployment benefits since they were paying out the 12 weeks on a schedule rather than all at once. I had the weekend to decide; then Monday would be my last day. I could decide not to take the package and attempt the second PIP. If I failed, I would be fired with no severance. It was a no brainer.

By noon Monday, they cut me off from the network, shutting me out of my email and even the computer sitting on my desk. I was unable to retrieve all my personal files or reach out to key customers to let them know I was leaving. My boss never spoke to me again— never asked for information about my accounts, telling HR he knew everything about my territory and didn't need to speak to me. To imply I had nothing more to offer after 12 years felt like a final slap in the face. I had brought the company over $50M in revenue, often carrying one of the highest quotas and growth numbers of any sales rep.

Powerful women know that when your contribution and achievements are not recognized or appreciated, and the company is pushing an unrealistic workload to break you down, it's time to move on from a toxic environment.

Getting over it

By the time the day was over on Monday, I felt like an enormous weight had been lifted off my chest, and I could breathe again. The company had been a toxic environment for me for many years, and I just tried to ignore it and plow on through. The past few weeks had been pure hell, trying to satisfy their ridiculous PIP while knowing I needed to find another job but having barely any time to look or even eat.

I was still plenty angry, but I knew I needed to get on with it and find another job as soon as possible. I immediately activated my network. I contacted my coworkers from the past 12 years at the company and told them I was leaving, asking them to refer any job leads to me. There was a great outpouring of support (or its evil twin—love of gossip) from my colleagues wanting to know what had happened. The company doesn't come out looking good in the story for how they treated me, though people will believe what they will about whether I was at fault. I *was* partly at fault, of course. I should have left years earlier, before they killed my mojo or I just let it die.

By Thursday, I had shaken off some of the anger and focused on the job search. I contacted everyone I knew on LinkedIn. I had already updated my resume, so I sent it out to a few people who asked. I even contacted a few former customers, one of whom told me about an exciting opportunity he wanted to meet with me to discuss. It was selling Amway cleaning products. I took a pass.

Finding the positive

Once again, I had the opportunity to look for the positive in my situation. There was plenty to find. Mostly, I saw the sudden lack of negative. Nobody was telling me I was a failure for not getting enough customers to agree to meet with me. Nobody was actively trying to make my life miserable enough to quit. They took that decision from me, and for that I am eternally grateful.

I cleaned out my office, throwing away piles of literature, notes, and customer information that they apparently didn't need any more. I gathered up the customer giveaways from my garage and met a former colleague for lunch to hand them over, since I didn't want them. I moved everything into the center of the room and painted my office a beautiful blue with white trim—the first time I had painted that room since moving in 20 years earlier. I added cheery art on the walls and set up one desk for writing and one for the job hunt.

I was thankful for the job I had had for 12 years, as it afforded me the time, flexibility, and work from home that got me through my children's teenage years. It helped fund their college and my retirement. I had tucked away savings and could easily live on the 60% for three months. I gained lots of experience in sales to major and small accounts, government and commercial. I made huge deals and helped small businesses get started. I loved my customers and what I was selling. There was a lot of gratification along the way.

I spent the next three months writing, job searching, and enjoying life. Sadly, my father passed away during that time, but I was grateful to have the time off to spend with my mother as we made funeral arrangements. I received my current job offer while in town with her planning Dad's funeral. I started my new job on the last day of my severance pay. It all works out.

How do you recover?

Everyone is different. We all go through bad experiences and find our way out of them in our own ways. I have had plenty of setbacks, and I like to think I'm getting better at recovering from them. For me, what helps is reflecting and finding the positive in each situation, so I don't get bogged down in anger and sadness. I know I sound bitter when talking about that last job, but honestly, I barely give them a thought anymore. When I do, it's like my first boyfriend. When we broke up, I was sure I would be sad forever and think about him for the rest of my life. Nope. He's just a distant memory, and I barely remember what was good or bad about the experience.

When Valerie received a demotion at age 20 for not sleeping with her boss, she didn't know what to do about it. She took the demotion and later quit. "I just moved on. This isn't for me." Valerie learned from early on to separate business from personal. She had to learn to handle unwelcome advances gracefully. Now as a VP in a large insurance company, she frequently entertains clients. She tries to make sure there are other men along, so it is clearly a business situation. "What do you do when you've got a client that's coming in from out of town, and they get flirty? You can't piss off the client, so you have to handle it very delicately, just sort of back away. Be polite."

When Becky had problems with the new VP, she fought at first but eventually realized she needed to go for her own sanity. She was confident in her own abilities and saw that what was happening would hurt her career. Her ability to make that choice and to bounce back quickly were skills she learned the hard way. "These are challenges that teach you that hard work will pay off. I got rejected three times when applying to schools for master's degrees. I worked hard but was not a good tester. I had a man at one school look me in the eye and say, 'You'll never get a master's degree. You'll never get one here.' Once I got my master's degree, I wanted to send it to him."

Becky wasn't going to let others dictate to her whether she would succeed or not.

When Connie lost her job because the new guy felt threatened by her, she had seen it coming. She kept her cool even as her long-time boss and supposed friend fired her and told her he was "vicariously in love" with her. As angry and frustrated as she was, she knew she was right. She took her experience to a better work environment and had a successful career.

We have all suffered defeats at one level or another. We have all found our way to recovery and a better place.

Step by step

Getting over the loss of a job or promotion or some other defeat may require a mourning process. If you like having a plan, here is one to consider:

1. Wallow in self-pity if you must. Set a time limit, though—perhaps a day or a week. Don't let it go on too long, or you will not be able to move on.

2. Be angry if you must. Figure out who you are angry at and why. Yell and scream in the comfort of your own home or vent to friends who can take it. Again, set a time limit, so anger doesn't define you.

3. Figure out what *you* could have done differently. Oh, I know this is hard. Blaming others is much easier. But figuring out your own mistakes so you can learn from them is much more instructive. You don't have to tell others about them if you don't want (or if you

don't write a book about it), but be honest with yourself.

4. Forgive yourself. Nobody is perfect, and chances are, your mistakes are minor in comparison to the price you paid. Revisit the anger for a moment if it helps.

5. Find the positive. Surely not everything about your experience was awful. If it was, then find the lesson learned from it.

6. Make a plan for moving on. Set goals for when you will start looking for another job if you need to, and how much time or effort you will put into that. Include in your plan being kind to yourself—perhaps a vacation, a massage, or just a glass of wine with a friend.

7. Do it. Move on and don't look back.

8. Try not to repeat your mistakes or get into a similar situation. Use your lessons to help you screen out companies where you may be treated the same way.

9. The next time you experience a setback, go back to number 1.

Happy endings

I am now in the best job I've ever had. I feel respected and valued by my colleagues and management. I still work from home but am connected closely with my company and coworkers. The CEO has told me he is shocked the previous company let me go, as he thinks I'm the best salesperson he's ever met. My closest coworker—an engineer who travels with me and supports my accounts—is top notch, funny, and supportive; we have a strong mutual respect. His wife and I get along great as well. I have hired and mentored other women, who are surprised and gratified by the supportive and positive atmosphere. I've been so successful at this company, I've moved up to regional sales manager and play a key role in the sales organization.

I'm not sure if and when the next setback will occur, but I am grateful to be where I am now and am prepared for whatever comes my way.

Strength and resilience

If my career path had not included setbacks, challenges, failures, wrong turns, and multiple chances to recover, I don't know who I would be. As painful as the experiences can be, there is something enormously satisfying and empowering in getting through it and moving on to the next thing.

I found my own strength when I most needed it. I learned that bad can always get worse, but eventually things will get better, one way or another. I learned from my own mistakes and learned to forgive others who treated me unfairly. Some of my "wrong turns" ended up being right turns after all. I am where I am meant to be. I am proud of being able to model for my children how to recover from setbacks and remain optimistic. No matter what happens to you during your career, you can learn, grow, and leverage your hard-earned strength to propel you forward—and you may be surprised by how fulfilled you are by the experience.

CHAPTER 17

HELPING OTHERS

NONE OF US would be where we are today if it weren't for the women before us fighting for our rights, blazing trails, breaking ceilings, upsetting the status quo. I am grateful for every suffragist and women's rights activist who helped us get even the right to vote and go to work, as well as those who fought and continue to fight for equal pay and non-discrimination. Not long ago, women were fired for becoming pregnant or not allowed to work once they married.

Beyond those fighting in the courts and halls of Congress are the women every day in the workplace proving that we have something valuable to contribute—proving that we can take our places alongside men, and we can lead men and women to even greater accomplishments. Incumbent on all of us, in gratitude for those who came before, is the responsibility to help others. We need to guide and mentor women and help them navigate their careers. We need to speak up when we see injustices rather than let things slide. We need to educate men and women in the workplace about how to treat each other with respect, dignity, and fairness.

To be fair, not everyone is up for mentoring others. Sometimes we can only take care of ourselves and our own careers. There is nothing wrong with that. In fact, if all you do is model for other women how to achieve success—simply by being a successful woman yourself—you are doing a lot. If you manage that while taking on challenges, treating others with respect, and maintaining a positive attitude, you are helping women. If you overcome obstacles and find your way back to success, you are breaking new ground, and others see that.

We all need to know how to fight the battles that are still before us. The women profiled in this book offer the following additional advice:

Anne

Save emails. I'm a person who saves emails. I respond to you in an email, in writing, but I also look at it again before I hit send and don't just send it off in emotion. Set up your case. That's how I've maneuvered my life in the business world.

Speak your mind. I've never had trouble with men in the work environment, because I speak my mind. Don't try to hold this against me, because I've got emails on you. I was always very businesslike and straightforward. You're not gonna give me this? I'm gonna leave and do something else 'til you realize how good I really am.

Lynn

Always work from a position of integrity and do your best. We really have to work twice as hard as men. Anyone who doesn't think that is wrong. Details matter.

Make sure you have integrity and competence.

Know who you are. Takes a while to figure it out sometimes.

Have confidence in yourself.

Fight back in a way that's not an overt attack. Some politics are involved.

Figure out your circle of influence and don't go beyond it.

Be good at what you do, whatever choice you make. Must be able to maintain that 110%.

Don't take it personally.

You don't have to take negative things on board if they are not valid or well founded. Consider what is said and see what is real that you need to address.

Valerie

Command a presence. A lot of executives are tall with deep voices. They command a presence when in the room. Women often don't command the same presence even if taller. For short women, the problem is even worse. Physical stature makes a difference. Stand when you're speaking. Put more effort into trying to dress sharply. I often stand when I speak even if the men are not standing. Sit at the head of the table. If it's my meeting, I obviously sit at the head of the table. But still, if you really want to make an impact, sit at the head of the table and not on the side—definitely not on the sides of the rooms. Couple rooms where we have a table then chairs around the wall? If the women in my group sit around the wall, I make them come to the table. "But we have nothing to say." I tell them, "Sit at the table. I want them to see you sitting at the table."

Help each other. I have to help the women; otherwise they are just gonna get run over. And these things are not necessarily natural for them. I've learned through hard knocks. But I feel like this generation coming behind me doesn't know those things. Somehow we've given the impression that discrimination and sexual harassment are over. They are not. Even in our company, which is all about compliance and is against sexual harassment, and there are lots of rules and reporting mechanisms, people get fired. But still, it's there. Even in a subtle way, it's there.

Take back the hard problems. I recently had dinner with one of my key customers, their president, CIO, and lawyer. We talked about all kinds of stuff: CIO stuff, business, family, kids. The next night they sat with my boss at dinner. When my boss came back, he talked about what the executives were telling him, and it was a totally different conversation. To me, "Everything is going so well; we have such a good relationship. We're working on this, working on that—such great partners." They told him the bad stuff. "Oh yeah, problems with desktop, IVR [interactive voice response], this system function." Why did they tell him the bad stuff and tell me everything was okay? I can't do my job if they don't tell me the bad stuff.

Customer not telling me bad stuff is "I don't want to upset the little woman"? That's tough. How do you deal with that? You can't fix that. Now, everything he said to me was true; everything he said to my boss was true. He wasn't making anything up or putting bias on things; he just didn't tell me everything. I asked my boss, "Did you ask different questions than I asked, or did he just think you were the one to fix things?" I'm still pondering that—what happened there? Maybe I didn't ask the right question. Whatever it was, I need to figure that out to get that info the next time. Or was it "level," that he thought he'd get something more out of the CIO? But I do the work. Ron walked into my office the next day and said "Here's the problem. What should we do?" and I said "I'll do it. I'll figure it out. I'll get a team together, and we'll analyze it and find what the problems are and fix them."

And what I did was immediately call their CIO and circled back around. "I understand you told Ron there were problems. I wanted you to know that I'm gonna work on that. You and I will start setting up meetings to discuss this." So I took it back. I find myself doing that a lot too, taking things back. I think women have to do that. We have to make an effort to take things, make them ours. Otherwise, men will take them and run with them, and you're left with nothing. It's the hard issues we need to tackle. Otherwise, you get relegated to busy work and roles that won't get you moved up. You're taking notes in the meeting instead of leading the meeting. You have to say, "I'll take on that meeting and set the agenda, and I'll set it up and do a presentation" so you're not in the corner taking notes. It's constantly proving yourself.

Rise above it. Million paper cuts. There is a lot of that. You can't complain directly about any of this. They set the tone, so you can't attack it—have to rise above it. Be professional; keep doing what you do, the right thing. If opportunities come along to socialize or interact, be professional, take them to dinner, take wives to dinner, whatever. Be respectful, professional, polite. And smile.

And stroke their ego.

I tell women who work for me, don't ever let them see you show emotion at work. Get up and walk out of the building. That's really important. You lose a lot when you do that.

Base everything on facts; have data with you to prove it, because nobody can argue with data.

Be fair to employees. Do what's right. Don't show favoritism to anybody. Have the same expectations for everyone.

Stay focused on work.

I tell the women working for me, if they have family issues, something going on at home that I need to know about, come tell me but don't make a big deal about it with everybody. That can backfire—I find people will make decisions about somebody, whether they are ready for a job, a promotion, whatever, if they know something is going on in their personal life. They'll say, "Oh, they shouldn't take that on; that's just more stress; they don't need that" versus letting them make that decision. It has happened to me before. "You don't need to take on these extra projects, because you've got a baby at home." Let me make that decision. It's not your decision to make. Give me the project. If I can't do it for some reason, I'll tell you.

I tell them, even though it shouldn't be that way, it's human nature and people will make those decisions for them. Best not to talk about it or say very little about it. When at work, do your work, so when those opportunities come along for special projects or recognition, you are not looked at as not capable of doing it for some personal reason. But they have to tell me about it so I know what's going on. They've got to trust me. I can help them navigate that.

Becky

Be professional. There's a time and place for being fun and carefree, just not at work or with work colleagues or customers.

Life is not fair. There are no guarantees, no shortage of jerks at work. You need to develop coping skills. The response to discrimination should be an open dialogue. "This isn't okay." Not that you run down the hall to HR, but you say, "This is unacceptable."

Be more confident and stable versus being at work out of control and emotional. Create confidence and strength in your own abilities to do the job rather than focusing on who's saying what or "This person did this." The small talk, jabbing? It's not helping you, not creating a good work environment. Creating an environment of unprofessional behavior, you will be labeled as a problem or gossiper or whatever—won't be able to climb the ladder, because now you are a stereotypical woman, gossiping. Not that men don't do it, but they don't get labeled that way.

I do feel women must work harder to prove their competence. It's still there. I have a problem with this a lot—I'm a small, young-looking woman who doesn't look her age. I come across as professional, but if you don't know me, it looks like I'm not old enough to be in the job I'm in, and people don't take me seriously. I don't know if it's looks or size, gender, or whatever. But as soon as I open my mouth to speak, and people see that I know what I'm doing, it's like "Oh," but it's that stereotype of the woman and then the age discrimination. That's why I went back to school. How many degrees do you have to throw at people to let them know that you know something?

I think, if anything, the environment has taught me, smart women win, eventually. The problem is you have to cut through the crap. That barrier is always there. You get it out of the way by your ability and building relationships, etc. Have values and credibility.

I want to be known as a professional person who can be trusted. I will get back to you if I say I will. Not everyone is a good person. I lead with trust. I'd rather be that way than cynical and nasty.

Assertive is key. You can be assertive and not a bitch; it's about the delivery. I was overly assertive and was labeled that way, not because I was bitchy, but I didn't have the delivery down when I was younger and under pressure. I had a wonderful boss when I got out of sales into more of a customer-facing, solutions-oriented role. The boss was like a father to me—good advice, direction, mentor. He said to me one day (I was in my early 30s), "You need to learn how to politely tell someone to go to hell and have them be happy to be on their way." I thought, *What?* But when you think about it, that's good communication. They are not going to be happy about it, but if you make it a win-win, it's a learned skill.

Stillness and calm are necessary. As women, we often get labeled as insecure, over-reactive, emotional. Let's be honest: the shit hits the fan at least once a day. In the past, when it would happen, I'd be on the phone overreacting, "What are we doing? Why? Why?" Now when something happens, I sit in my office for five minutes and say, "If I were this person, this is what I would want. I come up with two or three scenarios that may help the situation."

Take the time to regroup; then you can approach the problem with calm and control.

Put a new wrapper around being aggressive. I've been successful—take men's traits, put women's packaging around them: politeness, follow-through, humor, whatever. Put a new wrapper on being assertive and confident, where you don't walk into the room like a jackass: "I'm running the show." You greet people, you are kind, but you are doing the job.

Find a good mentor, not necessarily a formal program or life coach. Find someone 10 to 15 years older that you have something in common with, but you have to be open to hear it. You need to be groomed by older people. Lots of older people guided me. You are twenty-something, so smart, so great; you neglect to find a mentor—too busy working to evolve yourself. Take an hour a day—I usually do it over lunch, get out of my office—and think, really think about *What do I need to get done today? Is what I'm doing focusing on getting me wherever?* Lots of things we do today have no meaning.

You've got to detach emotionally. This is not who you are, and you shouldn't define yourself by your work. Just focus today on what you are doing and try to get it done.

You have to learn how to manage up. You will be more effective, because your boss knows what you are doing and why, and they are supportive.

Learn public speaking skills. No matter what you are doing, you will one day need to present in front of others. Join Toastmasters if that helps or find a public speaking course and practice.

Find your weaknesses. Your strengths are already strong. Work on your weaknesses.

Judy

Don't cry in the workplace. I had a mentor years ago who told me, "Don't do it. Take a bottle of water if you think it's going to be emotional. Take a sip. Take a deep breath. Don't even go there." Especially if you work for a male, they don't know how to deal with that. It's perceived as a weakness or irrational. I get teary eyed when I'm angry—that's how I express my anger sometimes. This is very frustrating, because it gets in the way of my being able to express what I want to express, but it's been years and years since I've cried in the workplace.

Don't ever use flirting to get what you want. I am no nonsense, and I try and be as non-sexual as I can. I don't wear provocative clothing. I don't flirt. I take it out of the workplace. I think people think I'm cold sometimes, but I have a reputation for getting things done, so I'm not worried about it.

Be supportive of other women. Celebrate their achievements with them rather than trying to knock them down a peg by talking about what they might not have done so well. Too often in business I see women undermine other women. I think by far that is one of the most destructive things for women in the workplace, being jealous It's okay to be jealous, but also be happy that women are advancing in the workspace. Celebrate each other. Help each other out. Men help each other out all the time in their informal networks and their beers and happy hours. We have to do the same for our gender.

Keep sex out of the workplace. Don't use your gender to sell. I see it with vendors all the time. They send in the "token female." And men know what's going on; I've heard them talk about it. One woman comes in, short skirts, makeup, flirtatiousness . . . "Let's go to lunch." I can't respect companies who put women in those roles with that intent. Plenty do it. It's disgusting. Women that stoop to that are discrediting the rest of us.

Rosa

Embrace your power. Women need to stop being afraid of power. You can't help others or yourself if you don't have power. Embrace power and teach your daughters to do the same.

Karen

Choose your battles. Save times of confrontation for when they are more effective. There comes a point where you have to say "No." I didn't start out this way. I used to be a doormat, not confront, go home and grumble—or worse, push it down until it would come exploding out. I worked with this woman whose favorite expression was, "I'm just gonna put it out there, just gonna say it." So to survive in that environment, you had to say what you thought back. I got that freedom to use my voice. I had the right to say, "I don't like it when you say that or do that." I don't think, as women, we are encouraged to do that, so when we do we're seen as bitches. I don't think they do it here, but at other companies, I know they talk about "the bitch in HR." If I were a man, I'd be a strong and powerful one, but since I'm female, I'm a bitch. And hey, so what? I'm a bitch. I've been called a lot worse.

Be your authentic self. Be intellectually curious. I use the "What happens when I poke this button?" approach. Don't let the boys tell you what you're not, because that's what boys do. They start on the playground, pulling your hair and hitting you. Mom tells you, "Oh, that's because he likes you." What's effed up about that, right? And you wonder how you get into an abusive relationship. Boys will tell you you're not fast enough, good enough, tall enough, you're not, you're not, you're not. Don't let them tell you that—not just the boys. Don't let anyone define who you are.

Practice your words over and over and over 'til they don't feel so strange. In the shower, in the car, in your head, practice your words until you are comfortable with them—especially if it is things you're not used to saying. One woman told me she had a woman in her office who criticized everything she did, then would say, "I'll just do it myself." I said, "What would happen if you said, 'I appreciate what you're doing, but I really want to learn to do this myself.'" "Well, I could never say that." "Why not?" "Might hurt her feelings." "She's hurting your feelings, and you're not going to do it in a way that's ugly." I say you practice your words over and over until it sounds natural, practice it out loud, to your husband, at home, over and over and over again until you claim the words.

Shirley

Learn how to work within the system. It's bigger than you, but you have a choice. Can you achieve what you want in this culture?

Learn what works best to get what you want from each individual you are working with. Some managers or coworkers will want all the details of what you are doing, and others just want the executive summary. The more you pay attention to what each person needs, the better you can tailor your responses.

Stay true to who you are. Make sure the company is right for you. Know your center. Do what calls to you. Be honest in a professional way.

Connie

Keep your integrity—that doesn't mean getting on your high horse. I understood what was going on and how things were deteriorating (like when he had me draw up a very detailed job description and marketing plan for the company and then told me that he never read it).

I should have removed myself from the situation earlier, but like I've heard from others, <u>sometimes you feel trapped</u>. That trap is multifactorial—trapped because you need the money, trapped because you're invested emotionally. I think that "trapped emotionally" thing is probably much more something that women feel. We have work relationships that we may not want to end, an emotional commitment to the company, etc. That was very much how I felt, anyway. I had been the first employee and played an integral part in designing the company's products and services. I should have divorced myself emotionally. I'm not sure I ever have. I still think about the whole situation.

Diana

<u>No one, NO ONE will care as much about your career as you, so take care of it yourself</u>. Do not wait for someone to look out for you. <u>Look out for yourself</u>. Don't wait for opportunity; make it. Men will not wait their turn or defer to those more senior with regard to opportunity; you shouldn't either.

Women underestimate their abilities and men overestimate them, and so they think they are ready for the next job—even if they aren't. *Stretch yourself.* Reach out beyond what is comfortable if you think you can do the job—or even if you think it will be a challenge. Successful women take on challenges.

YOU HAVE WHAT IT TAKES

Sheila

<u>Don't fall for the "female" roles</u>. We'd be in a meeting and I'm the only woman there, so they would expect me to take notes. I would always find ways to get out of that. I never was expected to go get the coffee, but they thought because I was a woman, I should be taking notes.

<u>Help others</u>. I was mentoring a young girl this past year; I really enjoyed that. She was bright, hard-working—appreciated my advice. It's nice to help younger women coming up.

<u>Look for ways to be a contributor</u>. Don't just do what you are expected to do—go beyond—male or female, maybe more so with female.

<u>Be a listener,</u> one of the greatest skills anyone can have. Don't just go throwing your opinion out all the time; take the time to listen to others rather than talking.

<u>Don't consider your job to be only the workplace</u>. Get involved outside your job in industry, networking. Start doing that early on. There are all kinds of industry associations you can join. Make a name for yourself. That can help if you need to change jobs down the road. I've done it more in the past—now with LinkedIn, one of the greatest tools. If you're not on LinkedIn and want to move around, it's going to be rough.

<u>Be an active participant in industry groups</u>, not just attending meetings. Try to take on a committee

role, make yourself known in the association. That opens the doors for you wider.

Learn how to negotiate for yourself. I have struggled with this one. When I took one job, I had been out of work a couple months. I was the major breadwinner. I remember we were out somewhere on the road. They called and made me an offer, and I said, "Sounds great." I knew I had made a mistake the minute I heard the HR person say, "Really?" I should have negotiated. Later I found out what a couple of my colleagues were making. I've never been good at negotiating for myself. I don't know how to get better at that. Somehow these women have to learn how to do this. Find out your worth in the marketplace and stand up for yourself.

Get additional training. Always be improving yourself.

Be careful not to overdo it. With startups, you end up doing more than you were hired to do; it's the nature of the beast. Maybe because I was single, I let it get out of control. I worked some stupid hours. Others were not working as hard. I was doing all manual billing; I should have stopped. As long as I was doing it every month, they had no incentive to fix it. I was taking care of things, killing myself in the process. I don't do that now; I've learned. I'm not a workaholic anymore, like I used to be. I finally realized it's not worth it.

Do what you like to do. You shouldn't feel you are not ambitious if you don't have those aspirations.

Don't worry about what your title is; just do what you like to do.

Advice from me

Keep the faith. This may seem daunting, when you consider all the challenges still out there in the workplace for women. But we are making strides, and each of us has the power to succeed. If we learn from each other and support each other, we can achieve great things.

Study, learn, and improve. Reading this book is a great start. Learn what has worked for others and see if it applies to your situation. Pay attention to your surroundings and listen to how others around you are talking. Even the greatest challenges can be an excellent learning experience.

Negotiate: Be your own best advocate. Don't accept the first job offer without considering whether there is room to negotiate. Ask for more money, more vacation, or whatever you think you will want and need. Studies show men negotiate much more than women, which may contribute to the pay gap. There's no harm in asking; it may show your new employer that you have negotiating skills, which can be very important.

Help each other. We are all in this together. Don't make it harder for the other women around you. Whom can you help along the way? How can you provide guidance and inspiration to others?

How much you benefit from helping others may surprise you.

Look for the positive and pick yourself up after defeat. There is always something to be gained from everything that happens to you. No decision—even a bad one—has to be a forever one. You can always make another decision later. Climbing a mountain is rarely a straight shot up—you would be exhausted if it were. Take the switchbacks and rest after you stumble. You can still get there.

Find your savvy. It's in there, waiting to be unlocked. Bring it out with confidence and get on with the business of succeeding.

CHAPTER 18

STARTING FROM WHERE YOU ARE

WE ALL START SOMEWHERE. Very few people were born with the proverbial silver spoon in their mouth. We all have to make our way forward from wherever we are, however we were raised, and whatever happened to us growing up.

Not all women are born with supportive parents and opportunities for education and advancement. Even those that were encounter challenges on the way that set them back. Others have established habits and reputations that are hard to move away from.

How do you use the advantages or disadvantages of how you were raised to work in your favor? How do you change what you have been doing all along? Even if you are mid-stream in your career, can you change your behaviors and others' perceptions of you? What are the obstacles, and how do you overcome them?

YOU HAVE WHAT IT TAKES

What your parents taught you

Some of what we bring to the workplace is how we were raised. This can be a good thing... or a challenge. I don't remember my dad's ever telling me I was pretty, though surely he must have, blue-eyed cutie with curly blond hair that I was. Instead, I remember his telling me I was smart, because that was what was important in my family. When I brought home straight As, Dad would pat me on the back and say, with a twinkle in his eye, "You do all right...for a girl." At first, I would huff and bristle about the qualifier but soon learned that Dad believed society's biases against smart women were as bogus as they were illogical.

Dad was a chemical engineer, Mom was a chemistry major, and their kids were into math and science in one way or another. My five brothers and I all went into computers or engineering. I was raised to believe that women could do anything. I was always college-bound and had only to decide what exciting career I wanted.

Whether that is a good or bad thing is somewhat irrelevant. I was used to being valued and succeeding in academics. When I ran into issues in the workplace, I was surprised and unprepared. If I had known to expect bias from the beginning, would it have been better? I don't think so.

And what if I'd had a completely different upbringing? Could I still have achieved success? Of course.

Rosa

I really was not raised by my parents and came from a very dysfunctional home. Both my parents pretty much abandoned their four kids. It truly is a miracle that I am where I am today. My grandmother, who was 72 when I turned 12, did the best she could, but we were exiles from our home country. My family was pretty wealthy there, and my parents did not expect to have to work or worry about taking care of themselves and pretty much never did. They were totally unprepared to take care of kids in the States. For most of my young life, I truly expected that we would be returning home soon. Unlike the others, I really don't know where I got the presence of mind to keep going.

Did Rosa's fighting spirit come from having to pull herself up by her bootstraps with no support from her family? She certainly didn't have the kind of support I did, but she learned to stand up for herself and fight for what she deserved.

Lynn

Lynn's fighting spirit and confidence came from a stricter upbringing. She was raised with eight girls and two boys in her family and went to Catholic school. All the siblings went to college.

One sister got married and didn't get her two-year degree. Others got master's and doctorates. We knew we were going to college. My dad became a pilot and got his degree in the Air Force. Mom had a two-year degree. The family was very competitive—military brats. My parents always taught me, "What you do, you do well. Work hard." It gave me confidence. I stood at attention at the wall if I got in trouble or was restricted to my room. With 10 kids, you had to have order, consequences if you did wrong. My parents never said, "You can't challenge authority." We could ask them questions; they encouraged us to learn more, find out what was right.

This is why I can take it when I hear that the bad rumors spread about me. I'm confident in myself. I will get to the source, see what's going on.

Diana

It was beaten into me, like a drumbeat, "Be financially independent. You work, you work, you achieve, you achieve, you get an education." Like a drumbeat, absolutely.

Diana's mother was successful and driven and expected the same from her daughter. Perhaps Diana's difficulty in believing she is successful—in spite of all evidence to the contrary—stems from that?

What if you are the first in your family to go to college, or the first woman to seek a career outside the home?

Sheila

I'm very different from my family. My sister didn't go to college—never wanted to. My mom didn't either. My dad always wanted me to go to college, and luckily I wanted to. I'm the one that left my home state. I've lived a very different life than my sister and mother. Dad was very encouraging of my intelligence and ambition.

It's funny: My mom was a secretary, and she would say, "I'm just a secretary." I would say, "Mom, a good secretary holds things together and has a very important role." It would bother me that she would say, "I'm just a secretary" like it wasn't a meaningful job. I can think of secretaries in our departments that I really appreciated.

Sheila got somewhat mixed messages from her family. Her father's encouragement helped her make the decision to go to college and seek a big career. And perhaps seeing her mother undervalue her own accomplishments inspired Sheila even further.

Shirley

Shirley had a similar experience with her family: "Dad always said, 'Go to college; get a graduate degree.'" He had not been successful financially or had any exposure to corporate life. She had to figure that out herself. "He always told me I needed to be financially independent—even more important as a woman."

Shirley's mom had no college education. She was very supportive and proud of Shirley but didn't model the path. "She was a secretary in the school system with no sense of self."

Valerie

Valerie grew up on a farm, raised by her mother after her father died when she was five. Valerie's mom always emphasized, "Work hard; study hard. Don't depend on other people to make decisions and do things for you. Be able to take care of yourself, because you never know what's going to happen in life."

Valerie's older sister also had troubles: "My sister's husband passed away when she had children at home. I saw that she had to raise three kids by herself. Same thing: always be able to take care of yourself; make good decisions."

So once you start doing that in life itself, you just sort of take it on and take it to work. I can make decisions all day long. It doesn't bother me at all, doesn't scare me. I don't sit there and go "Is this right? Is this wrong? Is it a good decision? What's gonna happen?" Just do it. I don't have to look back on it. Doesn't matter. Decision was made, and we move on. If we have to make another decision later, we'll do that. Keep going. I think that's what did it.

Valerie had no specific expectation of going to college or having a particular type of career. She found what she was interested in, got the education she needed to further her career, and made sure she was able to support herself along the way.

Karen

Karen came from a very different background:

I grew up in a household where female voices were not respected by my own mother, a second-generation American. I'm pure German. To her, in a German household, especially on a farm, male children were much more respected than female children. It's how she grew up; it's how I grew up. I learned at a very early age to get my little brother to say it was his idea; then it would be okay. "Oh, Joe thinks we should do this." "Oh, that's a great idea." You learn manipulation at a very young age.

I went to college. It was encouraged by my family. I didn't have a choice of where. My dad was a World War II vet who couldn't afford school. He got a football scholarship to a community college, but he wanted to go to the university. So we all went to the university—two brothers, one sister.

Mother dropped out of high school, worked on the farm. She felt inferior; this is the German way of doing things. She said, "I couldn't go to school, because I had kids." Turns out she dropped out at 15, could have gone to school any time before she got married. Then when my brother was in high school, he wanted her to study with him for GED. She kept making excuses. She had plenty of chances to finish, but she didn't.

This is why I'm so driven. Nobody gave me anything. If I wanted to learn about computers, I'd follow the computer guy around and ask questions. "What's this? What's that?" That intellectual curiosity—I think that's why I have done so well. Mom had no drive and was afraid of her own lack of ability. Mom was very smart—just underestimated herself. She ran all the budgets for the farm and ran a seed corn business and managed that and all the taxes. But I don't think there was ever a time in her life when she thought, *I'm smart.*

Connie

Connie found women devalued right in her home:

There was no history of college in my family. I knew that I wanted to go to college—but no precedent for it, no encouragement for it. I graduated high school, planned to go to university, things happened with financial aid, etc., decided to wait a year—going into dental hygiene. I worked for a year and took courses part time. My brother was a year behind. Mom said, "It's a good thing you are going to work; it's more important for your brother to go to college." That was the mentality. It wasn't important for me to go to college; it was important for my brother to go to college. I disagreed, but in her eyes, he needed it. The money went to him. I had to work and put myself through college.

There was never any encouragement to move ahead and do things, but that has spurred me on more than anything. I have never gotten encouragement from my family. That was my mother; she was never encouraging. Mother would say, "Connie, do you really think you want to do that?"

Even with—or in spite of—no encouragement from her family, Connie went on to get her degree and eventually an MBA.

Anne

Anne did receive encouragement from her family, as well as advice on how to handle some of the challenges that would come her way:

I come with a different perspective as a black woman. Growing up my parents told me, "There's always going to be racism." Sexism was one thing we didn't discuss, and I find it very interesting, because this is at the time of the Seventies with the civil rights movement and the women's movement with the burning of the bras and all that. In my home we really didn't pay attention to that, because the civil rights movement was more important. My mother always worked, my mother's mother always worked, my father always worked, and my father's mother always worked. All the children were expected to get an education and go forward.

I think that growing up, I never paid much attention to being female. I grew up with five brothers (and two sisters), and I was just as bossy as they were. It wasn't 'til I got into high school where I started competing with people. *Who's the smartest doing this, doing that?* I looked at it as I'm gonna do what I'm gonna do. I didn't recognize that they had some assumption that I couldn't do it. So I just thought, "That's just how boys are," because I had five brothers. I just spoke my mind.

I [worked for] a woman attorney when I was a paralegal. This woman I thought was absolutely fabulous. She had a strong personality, and she was very good. I used to talk to her about courtroom decorum. She wore pants. She was comfortable that way, very strong. She encouraged me to go to law school. She saw something in me that she recognized: "You're like a little fighter who won't accept the status quo." I didn't realize what her struggle was until I got to know her. Very smart woman. She had made partner. She never said there was anything that held her back. She was always encouraging to me to move forward, which I always loved.

My mother grew up—she was a nurse, taught nursing, was an accountant, was a guidance counselor for teenage mothers—she was always doing something. So in my world, women always worked. I think it benefitted me to always know it's going to be something. You try to do it with grace. There may be a time to go crazy; it might be when you go home but only if they really push you so far. Always know how to defend yourself, how to deal with that. I think when you walk into a situation and you kind of know that you expect something bad to happen, then when it doesn't, there's a big exhale, and you can say, "Oh, we're all human, and we can go on." But when you go into something expecting that, you're not really surprised when it happens. You're a little more prepared on how to handle it.

Where do we go from here?

We all come from somewhere. Some of us struggled more as children, and some were encouraged. Did the struggle prepare women for what they would face in the workplace, or is it better to come to the challenge with confidence that comes from being supported?

That is a study for another day. The fact is we don't get to choose where we come from. We simply have to pick ourselves up and make our own success, whatever our circumstances. The women I've interviewed have done just that. So can you.

Raising our children

Those of us raising children need to be mindful of the example we are setting, both for our girls and our boys. We may not be able to choose how we were raised, but we can help mold the future generations to be more open, tolerant, and equal. Teach your girls to be strong and to speak their minds. Teach your boys to be respectful and inclusive. In fact, teach your children of whatever gender to be strong, respectful, and fair. Show them that men and women can work together successfully.

But don't pretend that the path will be easy. If they come into the workplace from a completely sheltered existence, they may be floored by the first encounter with discrimination. The ideas and suggestions in this book can show what to look out for and how to handle different situations. Just as you teach them about "stranger danger" when they are small, you need to help them recognize when they are being treated poorly in the workplace.

Changing mid-stream

Hopefully, you have learned a lot by reading our stories and advice. Maybe you have learned from our mistakes or our successes. If you are already immersed in your career, you have developed your own habits and reactions to situations. What happens now if you try to apply these lessons in your own life? Will you be able to change others' perceptions of you? Do you need a fresh start?

As you have read, I have had to change myself multiple times over my career, as I learned what was working and what hurt me. I struggled with changing my negative attitudes to look for the positive, and in some cases had trouble convincing others I had changed. In my most recent situation, I needed a new job to establish myself as someone with a positive and forward-thinking attitude.

The change starts internally. Once you have decided where you want to improve, you get the help or training you need. Others will notice—or not, but if you know you are doing the right things, it will all work out.

Going on from here

Perhaps what you have realized from reading our stories is that the environment you are in is toxic. Maybe you hadn't noticed the large and small things indicating how women are treated, or you chose not to see them.

With your new understanding, you can decide how to proceed. You can use all the techniques we suggest: fight back, play the game, change the game, etc. The obstacles may be the same, but you have new ways to overcome them. You will recognize when you have become a threat to someone and see the tactics being used against you. You have new strategies for combatting those tactics and moving forward. You have looked closely at yourself and know your strengths and areas that need improvement. You have a better appreciation for the motivations of others and can find the win-win where it is possible. You know the laws there to protect you and whom to go to when you need help.

The key is to adopt a positive attitude. There is no reason you can't succeed, no matter where you are starting from. You are strong. You are savvy. You've got this.

ACKNOWLEDGEMENTS

For all the women profiled here who trusted me with your experiences—you are strong and amazing and I'm privileged to know you. There is so much more to you than what I capture here, but I hope I did your stories justice. The stories here are true. Though I've changed your names and identifying details to protect your careers, you know who you are. You can be proud of your contribution not only to your work but to future generations of women who can learn from your struggles and successes.

I am grateful for all the people throughout my career who supported me and believed in me—even those who ultimately fell short of perfection. Each step and misstep along the way taught me who I was and who I could be.

My deepest gratitude to David Hazard from ASCENT Publishing. You inspired me to write books, coached me through the long process, reminded me why I do this on top of my regular job, and helped me all along the path to publishing. This would not have happened without you.

I wrote this book over a period of more than a year, while working full-time, and in a variety of locations. From my home office, to the ASCENT writer's retreat in the Adirondacks, to Anam Cara Writer's and Artist's Retreat in Eyeries, Ireland, where I finished the last 5 chapters. Writer's retreats are such a blessing, to have focused time, inspiration, and guidance. Thank you to Sue Booth-Forbes at Anam Cara for taking such good care of me during my two weeks there. If you ever get the chance—go there!

Thank you to my early readers who gave valuable feedback: Melanie Hawley, Trey Kay, Kirsten Boyd Goldberg, Maija Rejman, Karen Luft, Candice Bostwick, Don Young, Lorraine Duvall, Cheryl Howarth, and Kathy Sebuck.

Thanks to Cyndy Porter with Success Thru Style who inspired me to publish the book as a means of furthering my passion toward helping women succeed. Your guidance in all things from style to marketing have proven invaluable.

Thanks to Katherine Metres Akbar with Your Edge for Success for the excellent proofreading on a very tight timeline.

For my mother, who is the strongest woman I know, and who always believed I had what it takes to succeed. For my daughter, who makes me proud every single day. I am so excited for your future.

MARY ELLEN CONNELLY

grew up as the only girl with five brothers, learning early on how to hold her own in male-dominated environments. She was taught that girls and women could do whatever they set their minds to, as long as they were willing and strong enough to take on all opposition. In this spirit, she dove into school work, achieving top grades and ultimately earning Bachelor's and Master's degrees in the very male-dominated field of Electrical Engineering at Virginia Tech and George Washington University. In the workplace, she discovered the large and small barriers women have to hurdle, especially as an engineer. She played the game, fought back, and more importantly changed the game as needed to keep moving forward in her career – while raising two children as a single mother.

After over a dozen years in engineering, Mary Ellen made the move to technical sales, and she currently leads the East Coast Sales organization for her Silicon-Valley-based software company. Looking back over her 30-plus year career, and talking with other women about their experiences, she realized that the lessons she learned along the way could help other women succeed in spite of the obstacles they will face in the workplace.

She is passionate about helping women find success at work. She believes that with a little guidance and support and a lot of commitment, women can achieve everything they desire.

Mary Ellen lives in Ashburn, Virginia, where she enjoys singing (jazz and modern choral music), swing dancing, writing, and spending time with her family

Made in the USA
Middletown, DE
10 December 2019

80440564R00169